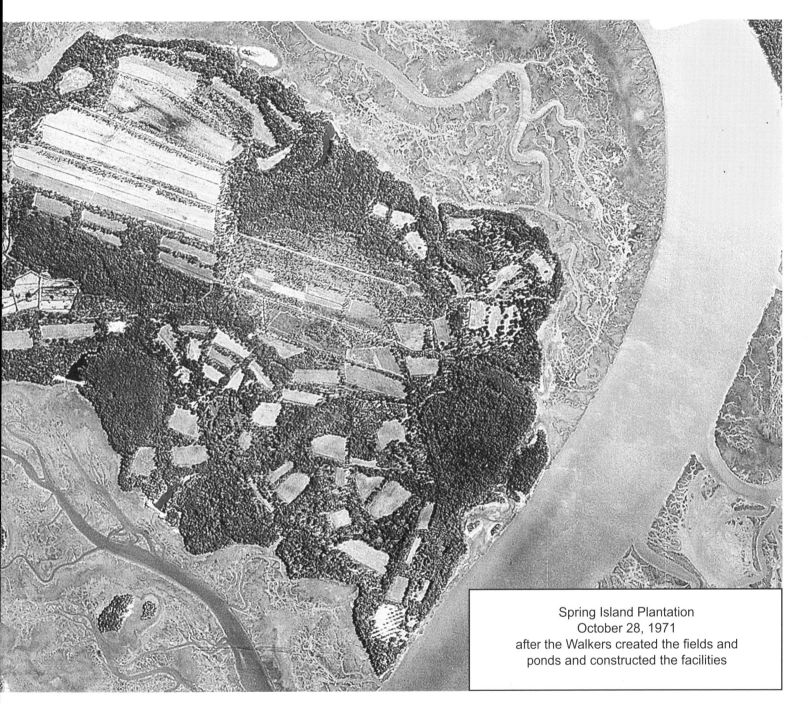

Spring Island Plantation
October 28, 1971
after the Walkers created the fields and
ponds and constructed the facilities

Spring Island Plantation
a remembrance

SPRING ISLAND

Spring Island Plantation
a remembrance

Lucile Walker Hays

Coastal Villages Press

Beaufort, South Carolina

Tabby Manse

Published by Coastal Villages Press,
a division of Tabby Manse, Inc.,
PO Box 6300, Beaufort, SC 29903
843-524-0075 fax 843-525-0000
http://www.coastal-villages-press.com

Available at special discounts for bulk purchases and sales
promotions from the publisher and your local bookseller.

ISBN 1-882943-23-6

First Edition
Printed in Canada

To my husband, Bill,
without you,
it would never have been written

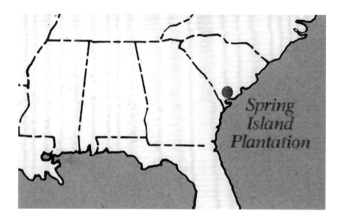

Spring
Island
Plantation

Contents

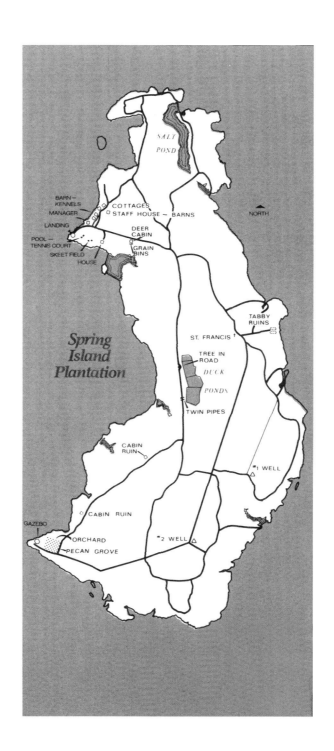

SALT
POND

BARN –
KENNELS

MANAGER

LANDING

POOL –
TENNIS COURT

SKEET FIELD

HOUSE

COTTAGES

STAFF HOUSE – BARNS

DEER
CABIN

GRAIN
BINS

NORTH

TABBY
RUINS

ST. FRANCIS

TREE IN
ROAD

DUCK

PONDS

TWIN PIPES

Spring
Island
Plantation

CABIN
RUIN

#1 WELL

CABIN RUIN

GAZEBO

ORCHARD

PECAN GROVE

#2 WELL

Introduction

The purpose of this book is to give the reader a feeling for Spring Island Plantation as the Walker family knew it. I have asked friends and family members who have visited over the years to share some of their memories, in one case a touching poem after a last house party before the sale of the island. I have included pictures from my mother's scrapbooks and recipes from my mother's cook, Flowers, and from our subsequent wonderful cook, Lee Maulden. Special thanks go to the Mobley family for their love of the island and of my parents. Together they all made a team that created the aura of Spring Island.

Lucile Thieriot Walker
1913–1982

Elisha Walker, Jr.
1911–1973

Spring Island Plantation
a remembrance

Opposite: William M. Copp in front of his house, 1930s.

The Copps

THE LAST OWNER to farm Spring Island before my parents purchased it was William M. Copp, who bought the property in 1920 for the sum of $55,700 from the estate of Alice M. Townsend. At my father's request in 1966, Agnes L. Baldwin wrote a comprehensive early history of the island, starting with John Cochran, Indian trader in 1706. It would appear that Mr. Copp had been actively involved with Spring Island for many years before his purchase, for recorded in the Beaufort County deed records is a lease dated May 20, 1912, from Alice M. Townsend to William M. Copp.

That the island was a working operation during the intervening years is confirmed by the following charming recollections of that period, written down by Nellie H. Fripp in the mid-1930s and preserved in the archives of Historic Beaufort Foundation:

An Island School

Girls, do you want some new kind of fun and a real thriller? Try teaching an Island school-while you are still young, or the magic won't work! I know!

Late one Sunday afternoon, September 30, 1911, as soon as the flood tide reached my little green and white row boat, I embarked for the enchanted isle four miles away, (yes, I could row in those days), and my adventures started.

A sudden thunderstorm burst, and my little boat was tossed about by the waves and blown off its course, close to the shore of a now dark wood. A loud squawk and flapping of wings made my heart jump in my throat, (I know, because I swallowed it), and one oar dropped from my stiff fingers! As my scattered wits hastily returned, and I grappled damply for the oar, the rudely awakened "Poor Joe" retreated to more private quarters, and the rain kindly passed in a white sheet, a few yards away!

When I finally stepped gingerly out on the muddy bank, near my destination, I nearly fell backward in

my boat again, for a pack of loudly baying dogs came bounding down the shore to meet me! They later turned out to be the most friendly of collies.

I first taught in the home of my patrons, a splendid Christian family. Then imagine my pride when they offered me the use of an old tenant house! I will tell you girls the best deodorant for this special breed of the house family! My helpful pupils and I liberally washed walls and floor with numerous buckets of salt water from the near-by river, then draped about green boughs of sweet smelling pine. A strong table, two long benches, and a chair for teacher, and an open fireplace made quite a cheerful setting, and believe me, this was no play school: Four grades, a High School pupil and all—not to mention singing lessons, Christmas plays, etc.

Those were among the happiest days of my life. Parties? Dances? No indeed. Some of my pupils and I would sometimes go for long horseback rides, or brisk walks into the lovely quiet woods, or cut for ourselves great stalks of delicious sugar cane from a near-by field, and the syrup boiling and sausage making! Wasn't it all fun! Best of all, I think, were the quiet evenings, when this lovely family all gathered around the big open fire to sing, tell stories, or simply dream.

And what did I buy with my first earnings?—a darling fat "marsh tacky" pony to help on our little farm at home.

I was somewhat "squashed" when the Negro "yard boy" informed me: "Dat horse never leabe dis islandt, where he born and rais, an he sho stamp de bottom outan any boat roun dese parts!"

However, I engaged the largest boat I could find, and a strong Negro to row. After much coaxing by my interested pupils and quite a large number of the Negro population, "Skip" was coaxed on board, and we embarked. I was holding fast to the bridle, a large package of sausage, and a black kitten which was given for good luck! Perhaps the little beast imparted its dread of water to the trembling pony, because "Skip" waited until we were across the deep channel

William M. Copp (left) aboard his steamer, c. 1910.

before he gave a mighty leap into the shallows, and plunged and snorted to shore!

When I finally bestrode my fiery steed for the two-mile ride home, I thanked my lucky stars (and the black kitten) that this great adventure was over—but no such luck! "Skip" seemed to be looking for ghosts in this strange new land, and when he caught a glimpse of a big white log in the tall "broom-grass", he gave a snort, braced his stout little front legs, and I was neatly dumped in the middle of the sandy road! It took me some time to decide I was not killed, coax the spitting kitten out of the woods, dig my sausage from the sand, and start limping home, leading the now subdued pony.

May I pause now to say, "Skip" was the best investment I ever made. He worked many years on the farm, was a "peach" of a saddle horse, and pulled my light buggy over many hundred miles of winding country roads.

A word about the Negroes on this funny island. Though strong and capable workers, they did not seem far removed from Africa in their language and customs. Sometimes, in our rambles, we would chance upon a bunch of scantly clothed black kids. They would stare spellbound for an instant, before disappearing silently into the thick undergrowth. I learned that most of these children had never left the island, and many had never seen a white face!

One night I was suddenly awakened by the most eerie and blood curdling yelling I have ever heard. The ghostly screams seemed to start far away, and kept coming nearer, until the whole immediate world seemed to be pulsing with the sound! Thinking we were all about to be scalped, or whatever it is cannibals do to their dainties, I hastily wakened my sleepy bedfellow. She listened drowsily a minute, then said indifferently: "Oh, that is just the grapevine telegraph sending a death message."

We found next morning, "Red Bird", the yard boy's cousin, had died on a neighboring island about six miles away.

One memorable weekend, and on several other occasions, in fact, my mischievous pupils decided they would keep me on the Island by hiding my oars! But on this particular Saturday, having urgent plans of my own at home, I did not stop to argue the point, but hoisted my little sail and was off in a twinkle. I thrilled at the tug of the sheet rope, the ripple of the water on the bow, and the flying salt spray from the white-capped waves, until CRACK! The mast broke, and the little boat nearly capsized. As I had no oars or anchor, I was helpless against the west gale and ebb tide, which swept me toward the nearby ocean. Not a soul in sight, until, joy! They had seen me from the Island. Two sturdy Negroes and the "boss" came swiftly to the rescue!

The end of this little tale? Believe it or not, "Teacher" and all her pupils are the happiest and proudest of husbands and wives, and there are just "oodles" of the sweetest kids! (Try an Island School)!

Nellie Fripp added a handwritten note in 1954, reading as follows:

> The above mentioned Island was Spring Island, on the Chechessee River, near the Fripp's Bluff plantation. At the time of this 1911 writing, it was a thriving truck and cattle plantation belonging to the late William M. Copp of New York. Now, 1954, it is completely deserted, except for animals. It belongs to a Mr. Lucas. Even the lumber has all been sold. The family mentioned were the late Mr. & Mrs. Porcher Pinckney and their seven fine children. Three live in or near Beaufort, one in Savannah, and three in Grahamville, S. C. The island referred to was Spring Island across from the John Fripp's Bluff plantation.

This explains why our mainland property was called Fripp's Landing and our island dock area was called Pinckney's Landing. Porcher Pinckney managed the island for Mr. Copp.

Mr. Copp constructed a large, two-story frame house with wonderful porches overlooking the

Aerial view of Copp House and dock with pecan grove behind; Mr. Copps' steamer is tied to the dock.

Copps House during the residency of Mr. and Mrs. Copp.

Colleton River. Known as the "Copp House", it was located at Bonny Shore where the Hendershot's house is today. Otillie M. Copp Mills, Mr. Copp's widow, sold the island in 1943 to Minnie E. Carter; she sold it to Percy A. Horswell in 1945; he sold it to Robert M. Lee, also in 1945; and he sold it to John F. Lucas in 1946. My mother found and saved these wonderful pictures of the Copps.

The following article, written by Chlotilde R. Martin, was given to my parents by their good friends Elliott and B Hutson. It is a framed original clipping that was published in the Charleston newspaper, *The News and Courier*, on January 4, 1931.

The Copps and Spring Island

This Beaufort isle with its single white couple, hundreds of Negro servitors, numerous birds, its orange trees and ruins of an old settlement is like something from a story book. Like something out of a story book is picturesque Spring Island on the Colleton River, down in Beaufort County. Like story-book characters, too, are Col. and Mrs. W. M. Copp, sole lord and lady of the island, and their several hundred dusky servitors.

From the time one enters their hospitable yacht, *Columbia*, at Copp's Landing on the mainland about fifteen miles from Ridgeland, until one pulls away from the dock on the return trip, watching this genial host and hostess and the shoreline of their island home fade into the distance, one feels under the spell of an enchantment. It is as though one had stepped out of the work-a-day world for a little while and sailed away to a magic isle.

The Copps are graciousness itself. This quality seems to rise intangibly at the first glimpse of the long yellow house with its wide porches and green

Mr. and Mrs. Copp playing with puppies.

Stairway and hall in Copp House

lawn that slopes down to the seawall, which has been recently built to prevent the wash of the river against the shore. And when the Copps come down their steps and along the dock, waving their hands in greeting, that sense of graciousness becomes a tangible thing.

Col. Copp is not a newcomer to Coastal South Carolina. He discovered it twenty-seven years ago and the lure of it wove its spell upon him, with the result that never again could he be long content away. He came down at first for the hunting and later became a member of the Spring Island Hunting Club, which was organized about thirty years ago by Col. Thomas Martin of Bluffton, who then owned the island.

Bought at Auction

There was a split-up in the Club later, and it was sold at public auction in Charleston in 1912, and Mr. Copp bought it. At first he was interested chiefly in the hunting, but later became concerned in making the island a paying proposition.

He began to clear land until there were 3,000 acres under cultivation and planted it to truck. He did an enormous trucking business, planting potatoes, lettuce, tomatoes, and other truck. One season on lettuce alone he cleared $60,000. However, Mr. Copp believes that the day of big truck crops in this section is over. This condition has been brought about by over-production and keen competition, he thinks. Due to improved machinery, he is now able to make three-fourths of the crop he used to make with one-fourth the number of men. Last year he received only one dollar for whole carloads of truck and shipped some at a total loss.

Now, Mr. Copp has turned his attention to cattle and hogs. He has about 200 head of Black Aberdeen Angus cattle and about 80 Hampshire brood sows. He hopes to ship between 400 and 500 hogs to northern markets in April.

In addition to his cattle, Mr. Copp is interested in planting grain and other foodstuffs. He has 250 acres of oats, 25 of turnips and two of cabbage, which are fed to the cattle, seven acres of pecan trees, from which he expects to ship a thousand pounds of nuts. He also dug 2,100 bushels of sweet potatoes this year.

The island comprises some six thousand five hundred acres of land and is plentifully stocked with game. Mr. Copp says he believes there are more birds on Spring Island than any other place in the world of its size. Wild turkeys are numerous; Mr. Copp said he saw 58 in one bunch while hunting on Thanksgiving Day. There used to be plenty of deer, but these have gradually left since so many cattle have been brought to the island. Mr. Copp says cattle and deer do not like each other and the deer swim away to other islands. The Copps also raise many chickens, ducks, and sheep.

Mr. Copp has his own sawmill and planing mill. Lumber for his house, built four years ago, was cut from trees on the island and finished at his mill. There are also a grits mill and a rice mill. Some rice

Mr. and Mrs. Copp in their living room.

Two ladies from Beaufort on a hunt at Spring Island: Margaret Scheper, holding a "picked bird", and Gladys Marscher, holding a turkey, c. 1930

is raised on the island, but is used mainly for baiting ducks.

Thirty-five Negro families live on the island and are all in the employ of Mr. Copp. All of these little tenant houses are painted red and the warm color is pleasant to see here and there among the green of the trees. Mr. and Mrs. Copp know all of the Negroes by name, even to the little piccaninnies who curtsy shyly as they pass along the road.

The Copp home is long and rambling and blends picturesquely into its island setting. There are two stories and two large porches which face the water. They have an ice plant, which manufactures 600 pounds of ice a day and an excellent cold storage. The walls are lined with row upon row of native meats and game. There are, also, an electric light plant, a speed boat which will take them to their landing, about eight miles away, in ten minutes, automobiles, both on the island and on the other side of the water, and even a telephone, which connects them with the outside world.

Large Orange Tree

At one side of their front door is a very large orange tree, from which, already this year, 14 bushels of oranges have been gathered. The tree is about 22 years old, and grew from a seed under the house, which stood on this site before Mr. Copp built his new home. It was bitten down by the frost one time, but revived and presents a lovely picture now with the brilliant yellow of its fruit bleaming (sic) through its waxy green leaves.

Mr. Copp is a man of the world. He is said to have been at one time one of the biggest lawyers in New York City. He is a Yale man, a great athlete and was a Colonel in the army. However, he grew tired of wandering about the world and his heart drew him to Coastal South Carolina. Mrs. Copp has lived in Pittsburgh, New York, and other northern points, but she says she never misses the life of the big city. About twice each year, the Copps leave their island for a visit to the north, and Savannah with its theaters is only a matter of thirty-two miles.

Aside from that they are quite content. Time passes quickly for them here. Mrs. Copp does not care for society, nor for the rush and push of many people. When they feel the need of other companionship, they have some friends down. But for the most part, they are happy here together. Mr. Copp is very much interested in his island and travels about it a great deal

Aerial view of the old barn during the Copp era.

by horse or afoot or by automobile. Mrs. Copp in breeches and boots, trails after him and is an excellent cattle woman, her husband praises.

They make a distinguished looking pair. Mr. Copp tall and straight with curling gray hair, laughing blue eyes and flashing white teeth. Mrs. Copp is also tall, handsomely modeled, fair and brim-ful of vitality.

The Copps live and enjoy life in the modern-day luxury of their island home and the casual visitor would not know that this is only a layer that covers up the luxuriance of a day that is gone.

Old Tabby Settlement

The mere parting of a few bushes is the lifting of a curtain, as it were, upon a stage dusty with the years and from which the actors have long since made their final exit.

Over a field and through a wood, and one stands still and, if he has not prepared, rubs his eyes for fear he is dreaming. For there, rising immense and white through the long avenue of oaks and palm trees is the great ruin of an old tabby settlement. The walls of the house are fully 150 feet long and three stories high. From its top windows, it is said, one could see far across the water into the town of Beaufort. There are also the ruins of the servants' quarters, a smoke house and a fourth tall narrow building which was, presumably, one of the outbuildings. All of these are of tabby and are perfectly intact. They are gaunt and white, except for the dark splashes made here and there by trailing vines. One has a feeling that if some miracle could be performed and the roofs and doors and windows should suddenly drop out of the air, into their proper places, the ruins would come alive again. A brooding stillness hangs over the place, that same stillness that lingers about forgotten gravestones.

It is another picture out of the storybook.

But time was when the big tabby house was a great mansion and the place teemed with life and was not shut away there across a plowed field and a wood that darkens in now like a heavy curtain.

That was the time when long staple cotton flourished "befo' de war." It was the home of George Edwards who is reported to have made around $100,000 a year on his cotton. Mr. Edwards spent his summers at Saratoga Springs, where he is said to have kept a racing stable. The story goes that he had two barges, one named the General Washington and the other the General Jackson, each manned by ten oars, which he used to make trips to Savannah. Sometimes, the old Negroes now living on the island have it from their parents, the slaves would steal the barges and make the trip to Savannah, a distance of 50 miles between dusk and daylight.

Burned by Sherman

The Edwards' was burned by Sherman on his march to the sea, and then the kindly woods and bushes hung the curtain to shut this gaunt memory of a former splendor away from prying eyes.

Mr. Edwards had one daughter, whom it is said, he disinherited because of her marriage to a British naval officer by the name of Inwood.

After Mr. Edwards' death, Spring Island was sold at public auction and bought by Mrs. Inwood, his daughter. At her death, it was her son, Trenham Inwood, who sold it to Colonel Martin.

While it was owned by Mr. Edwards, the island was divided into four plantations, Bonny Shore, Goose Pond, Old House, and Laurel Point. The Copps live at Bonny Shore and the old Edwards' home is at Old House. The Negroes of the island still divide it according to these plantations.

The island which is seven miles long and three and a half miles wide was originally a barony grant to Sir John Colleton. What other stratas of wealth or splendor have been buried here in the interim, no one has recorded. And what will be when time has rusted this civilization, which, at the click of a switch can bring the sound of voices thousands of miles away to this island home, there is none to say.

Tabby Ruins during the Copp era.

Opposite: Arriving at Spring Island.

The Early Years

For many years my parents, Elisha Walker, Jr., and Lucile Thieriot Walker, lived in Syosset, Long Island, where I grew up. However, I was born in Los Angeles, California in 1939. When my father went overseas in 1942 in the Army, my mother and I moved back to New York City to be near her parents and all the rest of both sides of the family. We lived in the City until my father's return in 1945. My parents did not see each other for three and a half years. Daddy wrote me all the time with pictures in place of many of the words as I could not read yet. His letters to my mother were all V-Mail, or small photocopies, but the ones to me were the originals. I am lucky still to have them all.

In 1945 we moved out to Oyster Bay, and after several moves, settled in Syosset. My sister Elaine was born in 1946, and Louise, called Weezie, in 1949. Weezie died in a tragic horse accident in 1959.

I went to Green Vale School through 9th grade, and then to Miss Porter's School in Farmington, Connecticut. After taking the two-year course at Katharine Gibbs School in Boston, I went to work in New York City. My first job was with the American Express Credit Card division the year it was created, 1959. My second job was as secretary to the president of the Vincent Astor Foundation, and I was fortunate to see Brooke Astor frequently. I then talked Frew Hall into hiring me at his travel agency and spent ten years as a travel agent. I loved the job as travel seemed to be in my blood—I think I was born wanting to see every corner of the world.

It was during this time, in November 1964, that my parents bought Spring Island from Mrs. Bertha E. Lucas of Charleston, widow of John F. Lucas. I did not spend a lot of time there in those years. Work and the excitement of New York City came before

Maud & Bayard Walker and Joe & Adele d'Assern, arriving at Spring Island, 1975. Bayard was one of Elisha Walker's brothers, and Adele was his only sister.

sitting on a remote island with my parents. In 1971 I met William H. Hays III, a widower with two daughters, Kitty who was thirteen, and Betsy who was eleven. It was love at first sight for all of us, and we were married five months later. In 1974 we were fortunate to find a spectacular corner of Nantucket and left New York to live in Nantucket permanently, a place that has been very special to every one in our family ever since.

My mother had one brother, Charles H. Thieriot, Jr., who lived in Locust Valley. My father and two of his brothers, Louis and Robert, commuted to Wall Street together every day. Their fourth brother, Bayard, lived in New York City and Easthampton. Their only sister, Adele Walker d'Assern, lived in

New York City and Litchfield, Connecticut. The four brothers operated a very diversified family investment company that included businesses such as a clothing manufacturer in California, supermarkets in Canada, coffee plantations in Paraguay, wildcat oil drilling operations, and one of the first computer companies, Scantlin Electronics. When I was twenty, my father invited me to accompany him on a wonderful trip to South America. He needed to check on the manager of the coffee farms that were not producing properly.

My parents enjoyed shooting in Quogue, on the eastern end of Long Island, with their good friends, Betty and Ed Greeff. Ed and my father had been roommates at Choate and remained close friends for life. Ed was a first cousin of Ethel Schniewind Pratt, wife of Sherman Pratt of Good Hope Plantation, and often went shooting there. Ed invited my parents to join him one year, and there began my father's love of the Lowcountry.

Ed remembered that one night over a good bottle of wine, my father said, "You know, I'm going to show you what a plantation ought to look like!"

Ed said, "Okay, as long as you ask me down." And after my parents bought Spring Island, he did—every year thereafter.

My father started inquiring about plantations for sale. He was put in touch with a management consultant for plantations, timberlands, and wildlife lands named William P. Baldwin. On July 5, 1964, a notice that Spring Island would be put up for auction was published in the newspaper. Mr. Baldwin found out that the Callawassie Island owner, a Walterboro pulpwood dealer, was going to be the prime contender in the bid-purchase of the island. He had unsuccessfully already offered $350,000 for Spring

Charlie Thieriot (Lucile Walker's brother) and his wife, Edie (Edna Hart Carpenter), at a house party on Spring Island, 1974.

Betty and Ed Greeff, close friends of Elisha and Lucile Walker, arriving at Spring Island, 1966.

FOR SALE
Bids Solicited Through Brokers Only

SPRING ISLAND

Beaufort County, South Carolina

Approximately 3,500 acres of high land **perfect** for retreat, farming, development, or game preserve. Substantial growing timber.

Terms: 10% deposit with bids
15% additional on settlement

Remainder over a three year period with a 5% mortgage without right to anticipate remainder on balance; right reserved to reject any and all bids. For further information, have your **broker** contact The Citizens and Southern National Bank of South Carolina, 46 Broad Street, Charleston, South Carolina, Attention: Trust Department.

Bids to be opened August 14th, 1964, at 12:00 P.M. in the Trust Department. Notification of acceptance or rejection by August 21, 12:00 P.M.

Island and had been turned down. He had just built the causeway from the mainland to Callawassie, and knew he could build one easily to Spring Island. He wanted the island for the timbering.

Baldwin also came across a 1961 story discussing the grandiose plans of a previous group of investors from Las Vegas. They had a contract signed May 15, 1961, to purchase the island for approximately two million dollars. They planned to subdivide it into nine thousand waterfront lots and restore the Copp House as their clubhouse. They were going to build shopping centers, hotels, motels, trailer parks, schools, and churches, as well as a golf course, yacht club, and marina, and provide wild game hunting and horseback riding. How they would have had room for the latter two, I cannot imagine! Their approach was not realistic but hints at the investment and speculative values inherent in this property. It also shows how fortunate we are that there were people willing to take the risk of a low impact, environmentally friendly development.

Another use for the island discussed around that time was to build a shortcut, called a scenic route, from Lemon Island to Hilton Head. The proposed route was to start from the southern end of the Lemon Island bridge, called the Dowling Bridge, and head directly to the intersection of 278 and Route 46 near Bluffton. Therefore, the road would have had to cross either Spring Island or Callawassie, or both. Financing for the project was to come from federal funds designated for "scenic highway routes." It was anticipated that this would create an economic boom in the county. Imagine, at that time 278 between 170 and the bridge to Hilton Head was two lanes, and there was nothing commercial on either side of the road.

Bill Baldwin wrote:

> Having lived and worked on many barrier islands, I can vouch personally for not only the unique charm of them, but the unusually high carrying capacity for game, acre-wise. So, what we are considering here is not a plantation or a quail-shooting plantation of the usual type, but a unique and hard to find all round wildlife area. The land is therefore not only valuable for investment purposes as salt-water "waterfront property", but could also be developed into one of the outstanding hunting preserves of the Southeast. It would be a veritable paradise for all types of game—deer, wild turkey, quail, duck, and stocked pheasant.

He also said that several members of nearby Okatee Club who worked in New York City were probably going to bid. So on August 14, 1964, Bill Baldwin put in the bid of $401,500 for Spring Island on behalf of my parents, and the Lucas heirs accepted it.

John Carswell tells me:

> My close and good friend Billy Morris from Augusta and I learned from the C&S Bank of South Carolina

Opposite: Copp House in 1965.

Trust Department that Spring Island was to be sold by them at bid. Billy, Harold Bishop (forester), and I landed at the Walker Landing, walked to the Copp House on the Colleton River and then back along the edge of a large boggy area, which is now part of the back nine holes of the golf course. Billy, the Callawassie owner, and Elisha Walker bid, with Elisha being the successful bidder, closing in November 1964.

The property was listed at the time as 6,036 acres, 3,600 of which were high land. There was, of course, no bridge to the island. Part of the purchase was a lot across the river in the Chechessee community with a dock and barge slip, our main access to the island. If you stand on the River House porch and look up the river to the right, you can see this area clearly.

Again, John Carswell relates:

> My first dealings with Elisha were with the Spring Island insurance, which we wrote, and secondly with a possible causeway at the current location of the Spring Island/Callawassie bridge. A contractor friend of mine, for whom I worked during the summers between college terms, offered to build a causeway with a large pipe where the small creeks join for $100,000. Elisha tried to buy a right of way across Callawassie from the owner. The owner refused to sell, but agreed to trade the right of way for the deer hunting rights on Spring Island, which he had prior to the Walker purchase. Elisha chose to keep riding on the boat and barge.

The first manager was Mr. J. P. Cooler. Because of inadequate progress, this manager was replaced by Wallace R. Stacy, a qualified forester from Walterboro who did a lot of timberland and wildlife management in Beaufort County, including work for John Trask, Sr., and Brantley Harvey, Sr. He came full time to the island in August of 1965, and

Above and opposite: boar ran wild on Spring Island in the 1960s.

a house was purchased at Fripp's Landing for Mr. Stacy and his family.

One of the first concerns was removal of all the cattle and hogs. A series of traps reduced the number of hogs quickly. Once, they caught two pigs in one trap. Mrs. Lucas had sold her barge so there was no way to remove them. Cattle prices were very low—local woods-run cattle were only bringing nine cents per pound. A barge was purchased soon thereafter, and then began the development of the island as an integrated timber-agricultural-hunting area. Within a year, more than $100,000 had been spent on capital improvements, including construction of a good road system and new docks on both the island and the mainland with drive-on ramp facilities for heavy equipment and timber products.

This tenant house still exists on Spring Island Drive, not far from Bonny Shore (photo by Jane Sampson).

Lucile Walker in front of another tenant house.

The only buildings on the island at the time were the old barn, which was to the right of the present River House, the Copp House at Bonny Shore, and several old tenants' cottages. The Tabby Ruins were completely overgrown and would need extensive clearing out and care. The island had been basically abandoned for more than twenty years, so there were no roads or fields, the docks were inadequate, and the Copp House was in very poor shape. Squatters had lived in it from time to time, the porch was falling off, and we were not allowed to go upstairs because it was dangerous. My father originally planned to save the Copp House and restore it to its former grandeur. He subsequently found that it would not be practical to rebuild it, and he had it torn down. I was not unhappy about this, as it would have been a long trip from the dock to the Copp House when you arrived with the groceries!

Having purchased the island, my parents rented a mobile home for the mainland landing, which served both as a place to stay and an office. They then put a huge operation into effect—new docks, a seawall, two bulldozers and other machinery working around the clock putting in roads, fields, fire lanes and dikes. Many of the roads are in the same locations today.

My cousin Bayard Walker and his friend Jim Davis spent about a month in 1965 helping to clear parts of the island, build causeways and dikes, dig ditches, pull roots from roads, etc. They kept a handwritten report of exactly what they did each day. To give you an idea of what was going on, here is one of them:

> This morning after staking out a few fire lanes with Mr. McCabe, we cut roots in the road for the remainder of the morning. This is one of the roads along the southeastern end of the island. In the afternoon, Mr. McCabe had to leave, so we took the Jeep and went back to cut roots for about an hour and a half. After that we took two of the cow and pig catchers (Mr. Cleland) around the island trying to get rid of the remaining cows.—JD

Elisha Walker on bulldozer, 1966.

In the margin next to this last sentence is written in red: "This against all instructions!"

The boys wrote that you could not see from one area of the Tabby Ruins to another because it was such a jungle. A report on this topic states: "We staked a straight line from the ruins, along the oak avenue, to the road. This took two and a half hours of hard work due to the amount of clearing that had to be done, just so we could see from one flag to another."

In the course of clearing, a few grave markers were found not far from the Tabby Ruins. One of them was Dolly Alston Hamilton who only lived from 1902 to 1927. My mother's two poodles, Grissette and Toto, are buried next to her, and some of our prize hunting dogs—Ring, Jet, and King—are buried nearby. Also nearby is the tombstone of Anthony Edwards, on which, insofar as legible, appears "C_. C." and, at the bottom, "21st U.S.C.T."

After the new dock was constructed on the island, my father erected an imposing flagpole, from which flew a large American flag. From the yardarms were flown his new island flag (a portrait of a gobbler), and the Seawanhaka Corinthian Yacht Club burgee. The main boat was always named *Gobbler*. In those days, there were CB radios and not cell phones. My father used the handle Gobbler One. Gordon, his manager, was Gobbler Two, and Gordon's wife, Janice, was Island Girl.

My parents invited their friend, architect Hans Seherr-Thoss of Litchfield, Connecticut, to design the apartment, office and garage on the mainland, two larger houses, and two small guesthouses for the island, and contracted Jim Rentz of Coastal Contractors in Beaufort to construct them. They built their house, which became known as the

Top: Gravestone of Anthony Edwards.

Bottom: Gravestone of Dolly Alston Hamilton; on left, grave markers of Lucile Walker's two poodles, Toto and Grissette.

Opposite: Lucile Walker at Tabby Ruins, 1966

38

Building roads, 1965.

Pinckney dock under construction, 1965.

Dike at Pine Island goes in, 1965.

Elisha Walker, Jim Rentz, contractor, and Hans Seherr-Thoss, architect.

Walker House, anticipating that it would be a future manager's residence when they moved to the Copp House. As they never moved, they enlarged and modified it two more times. After their deaths, when we started rentals, a new kitchen was added. When development began, the house was used as the initial clubhouse and was expanded several more times to meet that need. Now it is a private home again, so it has had quite a life!

The first night the Walkers slept in the house was March 19, 1966. My first time staying on the island was Easter in April of that year. A second house was built on the current site of the River House. It was intended to be the dog handler's house, so the kennels were located just behind it. In fact, it became the manager's house, as the dog handler became the manager!

Having the main houses in place, my father laid out the drive from the dock—first alongside the river, then past the new manager's house and the skeet field (now the recreation area), and continuing down to the end of our open fields. He decided it should be bordered with live oak trees. He was very excited about this project and told me he wanted to be remembered for planting this Oak Avenue, as Mr. Edwards is remembered for planting the avenue at the Tabby Ruins. He then had magnolias planted along the driveway from the Oak Avenue to the house, with two phoenix birds standing guard just before you turned the last corner.

The old barn and farming equipment were located just to the north of the manager's house. Past the old barn were the two small guest cottages, now moved near the art barn and called Little Cottages I and II. What is now the art barn was constructed as a quail holding facility that we called the Quail Motel. It

Flags being hoisted at the Spring Island dock with "Gobbler" flag on the right.

The Gobbler *tied up to the Spring Island dock.*

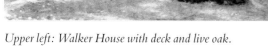

Upper left: Walker House with deck and live oak.

Lower left: Walker House with fountain.

Upper right: Magnolia drive leading from Walker House with phoenixes guarding the gate.

Middle right: Walker Oaks.

Lower right: Live oaks covered in Spanish moss on the path between the house and the skeet field.

Delivering heating oil to the island by barge.

First load of furniture arrives on barge.

got its name because it was a long, narrow building with a corridor on one side, looking into small rooms on the other side. Each room held hundreds of baby quail, bought the day they were born, and held to mature until put out into the wild.

The area between our house and the main dock was developed as a recreation area. First, outside the house was a large deck surrounding a magnificent live oak. From the deck, you crossed a little bridge over the stream that separated the house lawn from the beginning of my mother's camellia and azalea garden. There were about fifty camellias along a winding trail that led to what was our skeet field. In addition to a regulation field with high and low towers, there was a very high one. It was an old water tower that had been moved from the Copp House and was used to simulate dove shooting. In front of

the skeet range was a golf pitch and putt consisting of two greens and four tees. My father loved to play golf, so many a serious match took place there! The only eighteen-hole golf course in the area at the time was at Sea Pines on Hilton Head. He used to drag his manager, Gordon Mobley, down there once in a while, and Gordon hated to play golf!

In front of the golf area, bordering the road where the baseball diamond is now, was another of my mother's projects, an asparagus bed that produced quite well over the years.

A path led from the skeet field to our tennis court, and then the swimming pool, in almost the same place where they are today. Beyond the pool near the main dock was a shed originally built as a garage and a walk-in cooler, which later became the deer-skinning shed.

Old barn, spring 1966.

Quail motel and pens.

Small gazebo at shrimp pond.

One of the guest cottages built in 1966.

"Wild Turkey" by Wendell H. Gilley, Southwest Harbor, Maine. This was always the centerpiece of the dining room table.

Elisha Walker toasts stuffed island bobcat on the first night in the new house, 1966.

First Thanksgiving at Spring Island: Lucile Walker with her two daughters, Lucile and Elaine, 1966.

Lucile Walker and Grissette on the first night in the new house.

Elaine and Gordon Mobley at the skeet-field low tower.

Swimming pool area and tennis court (photo by Jane Sampson).

Lucile at the skeet field.

High tower at the skeet field with tennis courts in right background.

If you walked the other direction from our house, you came to the dike around the Shrimp Pond. A little gazebo was constructed where the dike turns the corner. It was intended to be a picnic site, and in perfect weather (no "no-see-ums") my mother would take her bridge ladies out for their afternoon game.

When my father gave up the idea of rehabilitating the Copp House, or building a main house on the southern end of the island, he hired Tom Stanley to design "The Gazebo" for Bonny Shore and implemented a program to take care of the pecan trees and the orchard. When the Mobley family went to Florida on a vacation to Disneyland, they brought back fruit trees to plant behind the pecan trees. The Gazebo was decorated with two large, cigar-store Indians and preserved animals from the island, including a bobcat, squirrels, and birds. The area was used for picnics. Lunch was served there once a week, and many wonderful oyster roasts and barbecues have been enjoyed there ever since.

My father, a spiritual man, decided he wanted a chapel on the island. I think he hoped to have a priest come over to say mass on Sunday. He had several building plans prepared. However, because of his love of the serene vista down the Edwards Oak Avenue, he settled on an outdoor chapel dedicated to his favorite saint, St. Francis of Assisi. He chose an Italian sculptor named Clemente Spampinato who was living in Sea Cliff, New York. Two pieces of pink marble were imported from Italy, one for the base of the statue and the other large, round one as a "meditation seat." Construction was completed in 1971, not long before my father's death. Our first service there was a combined dedication of the statue and memorial service for my father.

Elisha Walker carving dinner.

Opposite top left: Gazebo under construction.

Top right: Cigar-store Indian.

Bottom: Gazebo (photo by Jane Sampson).

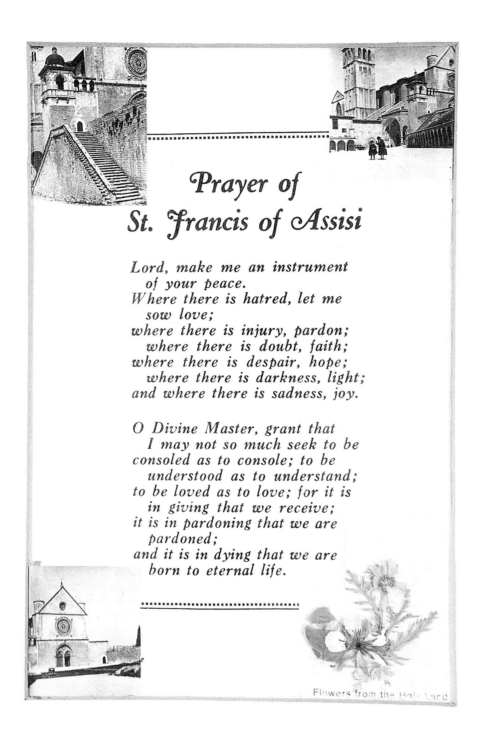

Prayer of
St. Francis of Assisi

Lord, make me an instrument
  of your peace.
Where there is hatred, let me
  sow love;
where there is injury, pardon;
  where there is doubt, faith;
where there is despair, hope;
  where there is darkness, light;
and where there is sadness, joy.

O Divine Master, grant that
  I may not so much seek to be
consoled as to console; to be
  understood as to understand;
to be loved as to love; for it is
  in giving that we receive;
it is in pardoning that we are
  pardoned;
and it is in dying that we are
  born to eternal life.

Flowers from the Holy Land

Above: St. Francis being installed, Elisha Walker watching.

Opposite: This copy of the prayer hung in Elisha Walker's dressing room with photos he took at Assisi and pressed flowers from the Holy Land.

St. Francis in 1973.

View from St. Francis toward Tabby Ruins (photo by Jane Sampson).

Opposite: Gordon Mobley with Spring Island buttons and bolo tie.

The Mobley Family

In 1966, WALLACE STACY, a qualified forester, was the plantation manager. My father determined that inasmuch as the timbering operations were fairly well established, and development of the island's agricultural potential was of paramount importance, a more experienced and qualified farm manager was needed. It was also time to hire a man experienced in buying and training dogs and handling horses. What was needed was someone to start from scratch to build a kennel and set up the whole operation related to bird dogs, including retrievers.

Bill Baldwin put ads in the newspapers in Charleston, Columbia, and Savannah. My father wrote and called friends in the area and in Georgia searching for two new employees. One person contacted was John Olin of Nilo Plantation, who put him in touch with his manager, Francis Frazier. Mr. Frazier recommended his assistant manager, Gordon Mobley.

On July 14, 1966, Gordon Mobley flew to New York City for an interview with my father at his 63 Wall Street office. I remember Gordon telling me that he forgot a jacket and had to go to Brooks Brothers to buy one before going for the interview.

On July 19, my father wrote to Bill Baldwin, "I have hired a dog trainer, farmer, or whatever you want to call him so don't do any more work on this point."

Gordon arrived on Spring Island on July 29,1966, with his wife, Janice, and their baby daughter, Donna. On November 3, my father wrote that Gordon was "just what the doctor ordered," and that he was a "personable young man and certainly gets things done. I believe he is really happy in his job, and I look forward to a long and happy association with him."

And indeed it was.

Gordon took meticulous care of the entire island—wildlife, dogs, horses, fields, forest, and, of course, the people. He seemed always to know who to get for exactly which job, and that often included his family, which was very large. He had eight brothers and two sisters. His brother Thomas moved to the Chechessee community and was in charge of the barge. Brothers Nease, Melvin, and George ran the family farm in Georgia and helped with farming questions, such as where to rent or buy equipment and where to get the best price for grain. Flint helped in buying horses, mules, and all the equipment to go with them. For instance, the harnesses for our mules were handmade by an old man who lived up in the mountains of North Carolina. Donna went with her father to pick them up, and the leather and brasses were absolutely beautiful. Joe Mobley was manager of Bull Island Plantation, which lies between Hilton Head and Bluffton. The owner was Lee Loomis, a friend of my father's from Long Island. Gordon's sister Juanita and brother Lamar owned and operated three restaurants in Waynesboro, Georgia, named Danny's Dairy Bar, Mobley's Cafeteria, and Lil' Chick. Sammy and Dale died young. Their sister Rosalee had been in a bad car accident when she was younger, and everybody took care of her.

One of the great traditions when we were visiting the island was to have a crab boil at Gordon's house. In fact, as soon as we arrived for the week, the first question was which night was it going to be? As na-

The Gordon Mobley family: Donna, Gordon, Pete, SaSa, and Janice, with Zibby (Elizabeth McBride) standing in front of them.

Lucile Walker cutting Gordon's shirt while his wife, Janice, enjoys the scene in the background.

tives of the South Carolina low country know, it is a ritual of covering the table with newspapers, and cooking the entire meal in one huge pot, including crab, shrimp, onions, potatoes, corn, and sausage. You eat the whole thing with only your fingers and a knife or a Coke bottle for cracking the crab claws. When we first learned how to eat crab, the most important people at the table were Gordon and Janice's three daughters: Donna, SaSa, and Pete. They taught us exactly how to crack, pick, and eat crab. The trickiest part is learning how to peel off the membrane around the chunk of meat in the body so that it remains in one piece, which they called an "ice cream cone".

Sadly, Gordon is no longer with us as he died suddenly in 1995. However, Janice and his three daughters have been kind enough to share some of their memories in these pages.

Janice Mobley Hill

During the years of the developing and growing of Spring Island Plantation (the late 1960s) after the arrival of and settling in of the current week's hunting guests, it was customary for Mr. and Mrs. Walker to host a cocktail party on the first night of the guests' week-long stay.

As a rule, though not at every gathering, the story of how Mr. Walker and Gordon met and became the team that they were would come up. This always delighted Mr. Walker, as this was one of his favorite "Gordon stories."

"Gordon stories" translated into introductory entertainment tales that Gordon, along with help and abetting from Mr. Walker, would relate to the guests: accounts of various and sundry "things"—for lack of a more descriptive term—that would occur daily as Gordon went about his job. For example, overseeing the bulldozers clearing fields after the timber crews had cut trees for pulpwood; working with his dogs; seeing to the care of the horses and mules by the hired attendants; duties too numerous to detail here.

The "how-we-met" story, of course, was never revealed to be concocted, to be merely entertainment, though in the end most guests and friends knew the real story. Now to get back to the story. If memory serves me well, there were two versions:

Gordon was driving along in the south Georgia area (actually the locale changed according to the

Lucile Walker and Gordon holding owl, 1978.

climate, particular guests, and whims of Mr. Walker and Gordon) when he came upon a Rolls Royce parked on the roadside. He stopped to see if he could be of any help. The car had run out of gas. And the rest, as they say, is history.

The other version is that Mr. Walker was driving (with or without his chauffeur), probably in the same locale, and came upon a car stopped along the side of the road—Gordon's favorite red Ford Fairlane—out of gas. And, again, the rest is history.

This, of course, is a condensation of the "how-we-met" story. Mr. Walker and Gordon would often parlay "the meeting" into a considerable portion of the evening's entertainment.

The following is the true story of how the Gordon Mobley family came to be part of Spring Island Plantation history:

Gordon Mobley was born, raised, and lived all of his life up to then in Waynesboro, Georgia. He trained to be a bird dog trainer under the guidance of Mr. Fred Bevan, who lived in Waynesboro. (By the way, a couple of Mr. Bevan's dogs won prizes at the Georgia Field Dog Trials, dogs trained and handled by Gordon.)

When I met Gordon, he was working the family farm business in Waynesboro during spring and summer. In fall and winter, he was training and handling the hunting dogs for Mr. John Olin (Winchester Gun Company) on his place south of Albany, Georgia.

Mr. Olin reversed the letters of his last name and called his Southern home the Nilo Plantation. Gordon worked for Mr. Olin at Nilo Plantation for two hunting seasons before we married, and we spent two more seasons there after our marriage.

Apparently, Mr. Walker and Mr. Olin were at least acquaintances, perhaps members of the same club, or maybe they had business connections. At any rate, from the best of my recollection, Mr. Walker told Mr. Olin of his buying an island and planning to make a hunting plantation of it.

Mr. Walker knew of Mr. Olin's place in south Georgia and asked about dog handlers/trainers, etc.

Mr. Olin apparently said he would see what he could do to help.

Mr. Olin told Mr. Walker that he had a good plantation manager and "dog man" and would pass the word along to him that Mr. Walker needed a trainer.

Mr. Olin's manager was a very nice man named Francis Frazier. Mr. Frazier, as I recall, liked Gordon very much and knew how capable he was. Mr. Frazier obviously told Gordon of this opportunity—and Gordon decided that he would go for it.

It's my personal belief that Mr. Frazier not only urged Gordon to pursue this position but actually recommended him—whether to Mr. Walker or to his representatives, I can't say.

Here, my memory fails me some. I'm not sure if Gordon called Mr. Walker's office or if Mr. Walker called Gordon. I'm inclined to think Mr. Frazier gave Mr. Walker's telephone number to Gordon and, therefore, Gordon called Mr. Walker.

After several telephone conversations, plans were made for Gordon and me to go to Spring Island, look it over, and see if this was what he wanted to do. We did. After a couple of more phone calls, Gordon flew to New York and met with Mr. Walker. This was the middle of the month of July 1966.

On July 29, 1966, the Gordon Mobley family (Gordon and I and our baby Donna) relocated from Burke County, Georgia, to Spring Island Plantation, Beaufort County, South Carolina. Within five years, we would add two more beautiful little Mobley girls, SaSa and Pete.

As a postscript, I'd like to add that, after all was said and done, as the saying goes, Mr. Olin was quoted as saying to Mr. Frazier, "I certainly didn't expect you to give away the best 'dog man' I've ever had."

Also, Mr. Walker later told us that Mr. Olin said something of the same order to him on one occasion (about hiring the best dog trainer he had ever known away from him).

Gordon and Rebel, Lucile Walker's favorite Brittany Spaniel.

Lucile Walker and Donna.

Donna Mobley Carter

Through the years, many folks have asked my sisters and me about growing up on Spring Island. Each response reflected the age and the moment we were in at the time. However, now that I am the mother of Emily and Josh, my own very active children, I am amazed that my sisters and I survived island life. I certainly believe God carefully watched over each of us.

I can't imagine the emotions my young mother experienced when she brought me, at ten months old, across the Chechessee River for the first time. Regardless of the weather, each and every trip to town began and ended with a boat ride, followed by a twenty-five minute trip by car. My parents were surely more organized, and we girls must have been healthier, than the babies of my children's generation. Otherwise, Daddy would have done little besides transport us back and forth across the river. And there was so much more for him to do. We did manage to grow up and have tons of fun in the process.

But more than the fun, the adventures, and the exploring, life on Spring Island afforded us the opportunity to grow up not only under our parents' love and supervision, but also under the watchful care of Mr. and Mrs. Walker.

Even as little girls, we knew it was our special job to take care of Spring Island for Mr. and Mrs. Walker. Our parents instilled in us at an early age a deep respect for the Walkers and for their island. Of course, it was an easy thing to do. It was their island, but it was our home. It is that sense of respect and reverence that I feel even now as I remember our early years. When you are entrusted to take care of something special for someone else, you tend to do it even more carefully, more faithfully, than you would for yourself. It was that way with Daddy, and with us girls.

Each of us girls would, over time, take our turns feeding dogs, horses, quail, ducks, and then shrimp. We each mowed grass, cleaned the pool, and washed vehicles and boats. We learned how to turn back beds for guests and to set out bedside ice water trays. Eventually, we each shopped and cooked, planned menus, and hosted dinners. The ease that we accomplished each task is evidence of the responsibility we felt to our father, to the Walkers, and to the island.

Of course, none of these jobs comes naturally. We were taught by our dad and our mom to care for the Walkers—to care for their island. Remember, children learn best by observing, not by simply hearing. Devotion to Spring Island and to the Walkers was a way of life for all of us. That means we went to Savannah with Momma to buy lamb chops from Smith Brothers; we watched as Mom rolled Mrs. Walker's hair; we postponed our dinner so Dad could tend to Mr. Walker's truck.

Donna bloodying a deer hunter's face.

An important part of our training included many visits to the "Big House"—Mr. and Mrs. Walker's home on Spring Island. Many evenings Daddy would come in from work and shower and change into his tweed jacket with the Spring Island buttons on it; then he would put on his Spring Island bolo tie. We had had an early bath and dinner and were also in clean clothes. Then we would load up in Daddy's green Land Rover and drive over to the "Big House"

Juanita Mobley, Gordon's sister.

to visit with the Walkers and their guests. This was their cocktail hour—though we didn't know it as such then. We girls were offered one cheese and cracker or a few goldfish or sugared pecans. And we had a ginger ale. Sometimes we were invited to choose a candy from an owl-shaped candy jar that Mr. Walker kept on a shelf in his room. Then we sat by the fire as the adults talked.

I have no memory of any of us ever being corrected in any way. We were taught to shake hands, look adults in the eye, and to speak when spoken to. Occasionally, Mrs. Walker would play a game with us. We would leave the room and she would hide her ring. It was a very narrow gold band that was almost impossible to find. There was much laughing and teasing as we searched for it. We knew these evenings were special. I'm sure we felt like young princesses in the king's court.

Over the years, we looked forward to the arrival of each of the Walkers' guests. It was like seeing old friends. Many of them brought surprises for us. I still have two ornaments on my Christmas tree that were gifts from that era. While Mrs. Walker had guests on the island for quail hunting, Mom and Dad would invite them to our house for a crab boil. That was another time my sisters and I would help out by cracking crab claws and creating "ice cream cones" for the guests.

I grew up somewhat of a tomboy. I loved all of the horses and dogs. Many a cold day, I could be found snuggled in the sweet hay of the dog boxes playing with one of the Brittany Spaniels, Reb, Opp, or Mugs. I looked forward to days when I could ride the hunt wagon and "help" with the horses. Mrs. Walker and her lady guests rode in the wagon pulled by meticulously groomed matching mules while the men rode on Tennessee walking horses, watching for the bird dogs to point. I was allowed to sit up front with Mr. Cooler and occasionally he would let me "drive". It seemed Mrs. Walker knew every bird, flower, and tree by name, and she taught them to me. It was only after I was an adult that I learned not

Donna on quail wagon.

everyone hunted this way. It was literally an everyday occurrence. How wonderful!

I have a special memory about Mr. Walker. I called him Uncle Elisha back then. Over Christmas holidays of, I think, my first-grade year, I was invited to visit Mr. Walker in New York City. I remember so clearly boarding the airplane. I was given a tour of the pilot's cockpit. He was an island friend, a deer hunter, I believe. My memory of New York is the vastness of the city. Mr. Walker's apartment had a bed hidden in the wall. That was something for this island girl to see. Mr. Walker took me ice-skating. We had a grand time.

During my high school years, I lived on Spring Island with just my dad. Mrs. Walker was living on the island full time by then. Daddy and I spent many evenings having dinner with Mrs. Walker. I didn't know it then, but God had put me in a private Academy of Fine Manners that would serve me well throughout my life. Looking back, I know that Mrs. Walker treated me as she would have a granddaughter. Many times I was given instruction in table etiquette. Those lessons were much more about the art of conversation and shaping my thought patterns than they were about how to use a soupspoon. Mrs. Walker took a keen interest in all aspects of my life. Prom dresses; boyfriends, horse shows, and school projects were all topics we shared.

There are many memories and stories waiting to be told. Each one will reflect the love, reverence, and devotion that I feel toward Mr. and Mrs. Walker and Spring Island because of what I was taught by my father. I teach my children that there are no accidents in life, that God has a plan and purpose for each one of us. There is no doubt that my family and I were greatly blessed to have the privilege of living on Spring Island and caring for the Walker family.

Daddy had a reputation for being a tremendous cook and entertainer. Simply put, he loved to host a party.

Many, many years ago, island friends Moose McLin and Hop Lucas teamed up with Daddy and William Fripp to create the first "meat in the hole" barbecue pit. A sandy area was chosen near the original tennis courts. A deep, gourd-shaped pit was dug. A pipe shaft angled diagonally provided air.

That first experience was quite exciting. Heated debates broke out over details such as the type of wood, how long to prepare the charcoal, and how long to cook the meat. It was an interesting prospect—to cook in the ground. Surely the Indians did

Gordon standing in the Gazebo.

Gordon and Harold Floyd pulling meat out of the hole with visiting children looking on.

such a thing. Many jokes were shared over whether it would even work.

Mrs. Walker was there to oversee all the procedures. She would unexpectedly drive up in her green Wagoneer to check on the progress. Mrs. Walker was always interested in everything that was going on. She was feisty and regularly gave her opinion. It was, after all, her island.

It was with much glee that we gathered around to unearth our intended dinner. Mrs. Walker, Daddy, Uncle Moose, and all of us kids circled around the hole, wondering what we would find underneath all that dirt. Daddy led us in a prayer-chant-dance sort of blessing (think Indian rain dance).

The experiment worked very well. The meat in the hole became a favorite way to offer a unique barbecue to island guests.

A meat in the hole pit was also dug at the generator shed at the Gazebo to facilitate entertaining at the other end of the island. Sometime along the way, we decided to relocate the pit to the walk-in cooler shed. (Skinning shed is a Chaffin-era term.) That way, the pit was protected from the weather and grass mowers.

Over the years, meat in the hole became Daddy's own cooking tradition. We girls were coached in the culinary art of preparing the meat. Copious amounts of garlic salt and black pepper were rubbed into the roasts that Daddy had ordered from Aunt Juanita's restaurant. We wrapped the meat in layers of heavy foil, so thick you would need shears to cut through it, then brown paper bags and heavy twine, followed by burlap, all soaked in water, then tied up with straightened coat hangers from the dry cleaners. Daddy built a fire in the hole around midnight so the coals would be ready at 5 A.M. The meat had to go in the hole then, or it wouldn't be ready at noon for lunch. One of our hair blow dryers was always commandeered to improve airflow to the fire. Imagine what our hair smelled like after a meat in the hole event.

As with most traditions, the "Blessing Dance" only got better with time. Young and old were coaxed into participating in the fun. Folks never ceased to be impressed at the sight of all that food coming up out of that hole. And it was truly delicious.

Fourth of July was one of Mrs. Walker's favorite holidays. After the festivities at the pool, we would go with Mrs. Walker (often she did not have out-of-town guests with her during this time of the year) to the Tabby Ruins to sit peacefully at the edge of the marsh and watch the fireworks from Parris Island. To little girls, it was magic.

Sara Anne "SaSa" Mobley

I have been asked to provide a story about growing up on Spring Island, something very difficult for me to do for many reasons. Since there are so many stories and memories, I'm going to just ramble on for a while.

Unfortunately, my memories of Mr. Walker are fuzzy as I was just four or five years old when he passed away. I do remember his pipe-I loved the smell of it, and I loved to watch him "pack" it with tobacco. I remember him smoking his pipe with Uncle Floyd, Mr. Adams, and Mr. Benziger. Even now, when I smell a pipe, I think of Mr. Walker and Uncle Floyd.

I also remember Mr. Walker's bedroom at the "Big House" as we once called it. I remember the glass shelves, the woodcarvings of birds, the porcelain statues, the coin collection, and the big E.W., Jr. initial on the spread. Everything was always in its place.

He was very, very tall—at least to a four-year-old. Mrs. Walker, on the other hand, I remember as petite. But that is probably my later memories of her rather than the earlier days. She was always so nice to us, "the Mobley girls." She was stern, also, but mostly nice.

Every time she went on a trip, she used to bring us

Opposite: Gordon and two Labrador Retrievers fetching ducks in duck pond.

68

a gift, not just to us girls, but to Daddy and Momma, too. Once when she went to Hawaii she brought us back hula skirts. I have to laugh when I think of the three of us standing in front of the fireplace at the Big House with those skirts and little bikini tops on, trying to do the hula dance. We must have been quite a sight.

One night a week, when she was on Spring Island, Mrs. Walker would come to our house for a crab boil. Of course, whoever was visiting her would come along as well. I loved this. Sure, we had to be on good behavior, but it was fun anyway. We got to play the "ring game" and play with Grissette, her poodle. This is also one of the reasons "the Mobley girls" do very well at picking out crabs—we would all rush to pick out "ice cream cones" of crab for Mrs. Walker. Of course, she picked out her own crabs, but if we could get her an "ice cream cone" first, well, that was special.

I mentioned the "ring game" and I'm sure that must sound strange, but let me explain. Mrs. Walker had this ring that was so incredibly thin. We would go into another room and she would hide it somewhere—on top of the lamp, on the fireplace poker, anywhere she could think of. Then we would come out and try to find it. Sometimes one of us would find it easily, but most of the time, we would search and search and search for it until we almost gave up. Then we might get some hints and the "you're getting hotter/colder" thing. We all loved to play this game, and I think Mrs. Walker liked it just as much.

Some years later we took a trip to Nantucket and Aunt Juanita was with us. We went to Ms. Lucile and Mr. Bill's daughter Kitty's wedding. After we left Nantucket, we stopped to pick up a U-Haul trailer and filled it with—can you guess? Ducks. Yes, ducks. At this point, Spring Island was being rented out by the week during hunting season, and, well, if you tell someone they can shoot ducks, there better be ducks for them to shoot. We were quite the sight, a station wagon pulling a trailer full of ducks. How, you ask, did the ducks survive? Well, Daddy just made nu-

merous holes in the trailer, and I think he even tore off some of the panels. What's wrong with that?

If I say we entertained on the island, I mean we entertained. People would come for a few days or a few weeks. Some from the airport, some just from the air—one of those sea planes landed in Chechessee Creek, right where the old docks used to be. People wanted to hunt. People wanted to fish. People wanted to party. I remember the cocktail parties after the dove shoots. I remember Sunday pool parties—Dr. Jenkins, Dr. Burris, the Hubbards, the Floyds, the McKinneys, the Murdaughs. The invitation list was always two or three pages long. We always had something for Memorial Day, Fourth of July, Labor Day, and especially Easter. Easter was extra special because there was an Easter egg hunt with prizes and everything. Momma would prepare (with the girls' help, of course) and Daddy would cook hot dogs, hamburgers, chicken, and corn on the cob. Everybody else would bring a dish. We even made homemade ice cream, and we would float the watermelons in the pool to keep them cool. And sometimes we would have "meat in the hole" and Daddy would lead the customary Indian Dance and prayer to make sure the meat was done before it was dug up.

When Mrs. Walker was on the island, she would always sit near the men's dressing room near the path to the tennis court because there was a big shade tree there, and the breeze always cooled. In the end, someone would always get thrown into the pool.

I loved Christmas on Spring Island. We would go into the woods with Daddy and find the perfect cedar tree. Daddy would cut it down, and then we girls would have to drag it out of the woods. When we were little, this was quite a sight. It was easier as we got older. Daddy also put Christmas lights on the big cedar tree in front of our house, dragging a long, orange extension cord across the grass and plugging it in through his office window. Our house was on the water facing the mainland, so the lights could be seen across the river—and the animals have to have a tree, too, right?

Above: Gordon boiling crabs.

Upper left: SaSa and Beau.

Lower left: Gordon's girls in hula skirts, Pete, SaSa, and Donna.
.

71

I remember Christmas at the Big House, too. I remember helping Mrs. Walker (or maybe watching) with her Christmas card box. It was a small card file box with names and addresses in it. We would make note of who sent her a Christmas card and what year it was. I also remember helping to decorate her tree with Waterford ornaments. Donna collects them now.

There are so many other memories; boat rides to go anywhere or do anything; filling two carts with groceries and picking the boxes from the pile at the old Winn-Dixie store to carry them in and coming home to dead low tide; counting the telephone poles in the water at night to get across the river; the time the lady went to the bathroom at a pool party and found a black snake waiting for her; cooking and serving the guests at the Big House; afternoon truck rides around the island with Daddy; Daddy's daily truck rides with Mrs. Walker; the night the Gazebo got robbed—by boat; horseback riding; riding up top in the huntin' wagon; riding the mules, with hay strings for a bridle; sleepovers in the old guest cottage with girlfriends; crab boils, crab boils, and more crab boils (still my favorite); Gottlieb's bakery in Savannah; that butcher's shop in Savannah with the gourmet foods where we used to go every week when Mrs. Walker was in town; the sunset views from the dining room table; the many people we met; the many friends we made; the family we shared.

I think I have rambled on for too long now. Growing up on Spring Island was very special to my sisters and me. Life was not always a bowl of cherries, but we each loved it, and I think each has gotten something different from it. My memories of Spring Island and the Walker family will always be held in a special place in my heart, close to Daddy.

Some memories of home from a little girl's heart:

Boat rides and hairdos don't mix.

Doesn't matter what kind of weather (fog, rain, hail, big lightning bolts flashing across the sky), you'd better be across the river by curfew.

Late for school every single day for all twelve years for all three girls.

Run out of gas? Just wait for the tide to carry you.

No boat lights plus no moon plus lots of fog equals lots of prayer 'til ya get to the other side.

The *Gobbler*; weekend deer hunts; hay bales.

Mr. Mike cooking a pig over a "Gordon-made" pit; late-night poker games

Pickup trucks full of deer dogs riding over on the barge.

First deer—lots of blood, missed deer, cut shirt.

Missed a "big one", lots of @#$#@.

The *best* Easter egg hunts.

Opening pool party; Spring Island corn on the grill; "meat in the hole;" Daddy's infamous "Indian Dance".

Dr. Arthur Jenkins family; Dr. A.G. Burris family.

Mrs. Walker's special table (you'd better not splash her!); the golden egg.

Daddy's white leather shoes and straw hat; Marco-polo.

The Walkers: Mrs. Walker and Beau; games of "find the ring" during the grown-ups' social hour; lessons on table etiquette; Mrs. Walker's "favorite" tree; the story about the squirrels and the nuts and the dining room table; riding in the green Wagoneer with Daddy as he drove Mrs. Walker around the island.

The Mobley girls: SaSa, Pete, and Donna.

Opposite: Elisha Walker's favorite Labrador Retriever, Jet.

Hunting and Farming

WHEN MY PARENTS first bought Spring Island, it had not been cultivated or lived on for more than twenty years. Consequently it had reverted to a wilderness. There were no roads remaining, the pine trees had reseeded themselves, and with the growth of vines and tropical plants, practically a jungle was the result. Wild cows, pigs, and deer abounded, causing the open areas to be nothing but barren ground. The old Copp House had been vandalized and had partially collapsed. The barn and most of the tenant houses were in ruins. Therefore, the job of recovering the island was tremendous.

The natural resources of the island made it a valuable property and a wise investment. The soil was excellent and, in the past, had produced many valuable crops without irrigation. Farming for cash crops was the planned major activity for the island and the basis for the economic future. A total of five hundred acres were cleared by 1970 and planted with crops of wheat, corn, and soybeans. The grain bins were installed with dryers and other equipment. The amount of timber was substantial, and therefore the income from cutting it helped to offset the high cost of re-establishing the farming.

The farming and timbering were both serious businesses and the prime economic resource on the island. Timber had to be cut to make the island productive and habitable. Farming was a good use of the land and was managed to provide habitat for wildlife. Thirteen miles of fire lanes were cut and many drainage outlets and culverts put in. Planning the location of dikes and the exact design for each one was a huge undertaking. In many places, salt-water ponds were created for fishing and shrimping; others were designed to attract and serve as habitat for all kinds of ducks, but especially mallards.

Specified areas were also developed for quail, turkey, and dove. As my father wanted the very best hunting for each species, he went to great lengths to find the right people to advise him of the best way to prepare the land.

John Carswell told me: "In about 1967, Elisha engaged Walter Rosene, noted quail biologist and author of *The Bobwhite Quail,* to lay out Spring Island for quail shooting."

Walter Rosene made his first report on the condition of the island in March of 1966. He recom-

Hauling timber from the island by barge.

Opposite: Elisha and Lucile Walker at dove shoot with Gordon Mobley assisting with gear, 1966.

mended extensive clearing, destroying grasses used for pasture in years past, burning in specified areas, and forest management. Small fields were cleared throughout much of the island and planted with crops and cover for quail.

In 1967, 2,500 eight-week-old quail were released in order to establish a wild population. Fifty pairs of wild quail also were released early the following spring. A report from February 1968 states: "If you are attempting to produce a native covey of quail on each 25 to 100 acres of land, depending on soil type, it means that each small block of land must have some unburned grass left immediately next to major roads and field edges. A logical method is to circle each bird patch or field edge with a fire lane to avoid burning all of the vegetation in each 25 to 100 acre block. These strategic sites can be left unburned for several years, until they commence choking up with dense vegetation and brush. They should then be burned, and adjacent sites left unburned."

The bird patches were carefully planted to ensure the quail would thrive—bicolor lespedeza (fifty thousand plants were ordered for winter 1966) and brown top millet were some of them. The project was quite successful. Whistling cock counts were conducted during the nesting period in the late spring. The whistling cock count in 1967 was thirty-four; in 1968, it was eighty-nine; in 1969, it was one hundred seven. Maps were prepared marking where each one was heard.

Gordon Mobley, with Moose McLin of the U. S. Soil and Conservation office, drained the bays, two large boggy areas south of the Tabby Ruins. These became the long cornfields. Ditches for irrigation were dug, and wide strips for pine trees and quail habitat were left between the fields. Some of the

Painting by Dick Bishop with island scenes surrounding Spring Island Plantation logo.

Hunting quail down a cornfield alley.

names were Quail Alley, Bird Alley, and Snake Alley. The cornfields were where all the dove shoots were held. There is a wonderful aerial view of the island in the River House that lays out all of the land and what it was or would become. It is a conservation plan map dated January 3, 1969. Every part of the island is designated marshland, woodland, cropland, or wildfowl land. The total acreage is listed as 5,634 with 2,789 of this being marshland. The areas designated wildlife lands are ponds and inlets.

Duck ponds were created in different areas of the island with special plantings that included, for instance, banana water lily and Delta duck potato. Duck holding pens were also built in various places. You can still see one at the north end near Pine Island. Meticulous reports were kept on pond salinity and algae control. One interesting passage in a report stated: "We must be mindful that the mallards released at Spring Island did far better than those released at similar sites at Combahee Plantation and Medway where lateness of release made the ducks too tame. The principal problem seems to be the matter of not keeping the mallard in the release pens too long. We have numerous predators which can pick up flightless ducks, but it is obvious that the ducks should be released on the ponds while they are still flightless, or at least just on the verge of flying."

To give you an idea of the challenges of operating Spring Island in 1966, the following is a report by Mr. Stacy, the manager at that time, to my father:

> One hundred acres pushed us at all times on the farming. All of our farm work overlapped in cultivating, fertilizing, planting and disking the one hundred acres plus all the bird fields. At times the weeds overtook the bird fields before we could get back to them

Duck blind on a winter morning.

Holding pen with net ceiling for mallards.

Lucile and Bill Hays in boat on pond.

Gordon Mobley and Lucile Walker fishing.

Gordon Mobley fishing, Harold Floyd watching.

because we were tooled up for another operation and could not cultivate at the needed times.

We expect another one hundred acres of fields to be added to the present one hundred acres we already have planted this year. We expect at least another fifty acres of cleared bird fields and possibly even one hundred acres of cleared bird fields and open areas that will need disking and planting in bird foods.

We will need another larger tractor to help us in farming this increased acreage mainly because we have a shorter farming season due to the bird hunting season. Most farmers disk their land in the winter so as to let the weeds and corn stalks rot in the winter rains. We cannot do this for it would not be conducive to quail hunting, etc.

I believe we will need ten colored men to keep up with the work that will have to be done each day.

Two men will be needed to look after the dogs and horses and help Gordon in the training of the dogs and holding the horses at the hunts. One man will be busy on the barge and boats most of the time. One man will be busy on predators and keeping the quail feeders full. One man will be busy keeping the grounds and flowers and misc. work for you and your guests. One man will be busy on the bulldozer and road scraper most of the time. Four men will be needed to keep the island in good shape, like keeping up dikes, culverts, roads, cutting brush along roads, piling up roots and branches in the duck ponds to burn, planting seed on roads and dikes, keeping all the machinery greased, washed and repaired. All the fire lanes need to be burned of the brush and trees piled up. Farming will be off and on all year or whenever possible. Fire lanes will need to be disked when all the refuse is burned and even now they will need to be all disked for prevention of fires for we will have a bad fire problem with all the weeds growing and no cows or hogs to eat and trample them down.

Today, the front nine holes of the golf course are laid out through some of the smaller quail hunting fields and duck ponds. When going from the second green to the third tee, you pass one of our old duck blinds that is in its original place, which used to be in the middle of a pond. The back nine holes are partly laid out up and down some of our old cornfields.

One of the most important birds in the beginning was the wild turkey. There were none. Bill Baldwin and several friends set about purchasing them for release. Some came from Palmetto Bluff; twenty pairs were given by a friend up North; and in later years, some came from Turkey Hill Plantation. Areas of the island were marked as the best habitat for turkeys and watering holes put in. We had wild turkey for Thanksgiving dinner after that. Another bird purchased for the island was the peacock—there were two that lived around our house, and they made so much noise!

Elisha Walker wearing jacket with needle point Spring Island Plantation logo.

Morgy Reichner and Dick Benziger with their turkeys, 1967.

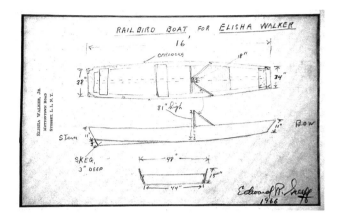

My father enjoyed railbird or marsh hen shooting and would come down with a friend when the season opened in September and the tide was right. In the beginning, he used a wooden rowboat with a small motor and a Whaler. Then his friend Ed Greeff created a special design for railbird boats for the island. He had two built and named them the Queen Elizabeth and the Queen Mary. They are strung up in the rafters in the Summer House. Look up next time you are there.

My father then decided he wanted a pin with a Spring Island emblem to award to guests for shooting on the island. An old friend from Long Island, Brinkley Smithers, recommended that he write to Richard E. Bishop. Elaine Walker Fiske writes:

> Visiting my parents sometime around 1966, I spent afternoons sitting on the dock dangling a baited drop line. The challenge was to get a crab to grab hold long enough to pull him up and drop him in a bucket. exciting entertainment for a Northern college kid who had never seen a live crab before. This was when we lived in a trailer on the mainland in the Chechessee community. It was later that a cinder block guest house/office was built on that site.
>
> It was after one of those afternoons that my father

suggested the idea of designing a logo for Spring Island, and he asked me for my ideas. I think I originally suggested a palmetto tree with a crab and a quail. He then hired Richard Bishop to design what became our family's official logo. It was used primarily for silver and gold pins given to guests who visited the island. The final version also had a wild turkey, duck, and dove. Today, it is a real treasure to own one of those original pins.

In a letter to Dick Bishop, my father wrote:

> We should have the state tree, the palmetto, at the center of the medal with appropriate birds around and, if possible, at the base a small crab and a small shrimp. The birds, of course, in the order of their importance on the island are quail, duck, dove, and turkey. This may make rather too 'busy' a medal, but I do think that if the various animals are not too large or too detailed it might work out."

I found in a later letter that they were glad they had dropped the shrimp.

The Spring Island logo today is similar to the original. Jim Chaffin of the Spring Island Company asked me if I would object to the use of our design by the Club. I asked that it be changed for that purpose, leaving the original for our family. It was simplified by deleting two birds—the dove and the quail—which made the design round.

Above: James Mitchell holding the horses while Graham McBride, Bill Hays, and Kitty McBride watch the hunt.

Opposite left: Design for railbird boat by Edward R. Greeff, 1966.

Opposite right: Comparison of Spring Island logo today (left) vs. Spring Island Plantation logo of the Walker family (right).

Above: Elisha Walker's Steuben crystal with his Spring Island Plantation logo (photograph by Jane Sampson).

Upper right: Original Spring Island Plantation logo on Walker family dinner plate.

Lower right: Modified logo on current-day Spring Island Club dinner plate.

Left to right: Charlie Delafield, Dick Bishop, Turner Slocum, and Carl Schmidlapp. Bishop designed the original Spring Island Plantation logo embroidered on the pillow.

From the very start, my mother organized her winter in August, sending out invitations to her friends for hunting season visits. Guests were invited to arrive Sunday afternoon and depart the following Saturday morning. They had five days of duck and quail shooting, and possibly a dove shoot, if the seasons coincided.

Quail hunting was conducted in time-honored fashion with a wonderful mule-drawn buggy or wagon made to order for my father. He ordered it from Bainbridge Machine Shop in Georgia. He searched the country for the best hunting dogs and retrievers, and we had some wonderful ones.

The wagon and horses would arrive at the house about 9 A.M., and I will never forget the first time I saw them approach. It was an impressive scene, one from an earlier era of Southern gentility and charm—the mules pulling a lovely yellow wagon with green leather seats and red trim on the huge wagon wheels; the driver with his red hat; Jet, my father's prized black Labrador, at his feet; the other dogs restless in their cages anticipating the day's hunt; and the horses following behind. This was quite a sight for a New York City girl! And off we would go, with a first down perhaps being across the road where the new barn is today.

Gordon Mobley ran the hunt, and B. Taylor drove the wagon. (In later years, it was driven by Marion Cooler.) William Fripp, who runs the hunt club today, was hired by my mother in 1976 and quickly became an indispensable part of not only the hunt, but all aspects of the plantation. James Mitchell held the horses while people were down shooting. The group would break for lunch—either back at the house or, every Thursday, at the Gazebo. That was the best lunch of the week as we had raw oysters on

Above: The original Spring Island Plantation logo embroidered on the pillow shown on page 89 is now preserved in this wood frame.

Opposite: Lucile Hays and Marion Cooler ready to go to the hunt in mule-drawn wagon, 1979.

Quail-hunting dogs on point.

Gordon Mobley holds dog while Lucile Hays shoots quail.

the half shell, steamed oysters, barbecued quail, and red rice. My father loved to cook and, being half French, was quite a chef. He had taken cooking classes in Paris and was a member of a French cooking group of rotisserie chefs called *Les Chaines des Rotisseurs*. He taught Gordon how to barbecue quail seasoned with *Herbes de Provence* purchased from Hediard in Paris.

As much as my mother enjoyed shooting (and she was a very good shot), at 5 P.M., she was always ready to quit and gave the order to pick up the dogs. One of the loveliest times of the day was the trip back to the house at dusk—the mules trotting along the dirt roads with their harnesses jingling, tired dogs quiet at last, and all of us snuggled in the wagon to keep warm.

Upper left: Lucile Walker and Jet after duck hunt, December 1966.

Upper right: Lucile Walker and Jet after coon hunt.

Lower right: Lucile Walker with dogs on point under Elisha Walker's oak trees.

At end of day, Marion Cooler driving quail hunters back to Walker House for dinner: Connie, Christian, George, and Claire Trask.

Deer hunts became another Spring Island tradition. Several were held each year, and my parents and Gordon would have a fun and varied crowd participating. They would all spend the night in and around the skinning shed near the main dock, playing cards and telling stories. An entire hog would be set to cook in a pit the night before the hunt. It took all night for it to cook and be ready to eat at noon the next day. After the deer hunt the next morning, they would have the big barbecue lunch. If anyone missed a shot at a deer and someone knew it, they were reported, and the consequence was that my mother would slit their shirt up the back. She had a great and gleeful time doing it, and I know that more than once, someone got their shirt cut when they did not really deserve it!

Dove season was great fun as dove shoots are wonderful social events. Plantation owners from Charleston to Savannah were invited and loved to come. Dove were plentiful, attracted by the big cornfields, and the shooting was challenging. People would arrive at the mainland dock at about 1 P.M. It was quite a process to ferry as many as forty shooters with families and dogs across the river, pile them into trucks, and deposit each person at a good station on the perimeter of one of the long fields. John Carswell says he and Bill Sprague always angled to be across from my mother as Gordon gave her the best spot. The shoot started at 2 P.M. Gordon would drive around all afternoon checking on everyone and giving encouragement. When I was at a dove shoot, I was out there until the very end, as Gordon would not pick you up until you shot your limit. Soaring and diving, wheeling and darting, doves are elusive targets.

Top: Elisha Walker cutting poor marksman's shirttail.

Bottom: Buddy Glenn and Lucile Walker eating lunch after deer hunt.

Top: End of a deer hunt.

Bottom: Lucile Walker cutting Buddy Glenn's shirt, 1973.

Bob Lamar's face is bloodied, 1973.

After the shoot, the crowd gathered at our house for a festive cocktail party with wonderful hors d'oeuvres such as sweet and sour shrimp, crab, and roast beef besides the usual cheese and vegetable trays. Some guests, who were non-shooters, would have arrived while we were out in the field. Among them were three ladies we all loved, Cora Lee Bull, Sallie Mae Hollins, and Helen Frances Stokes. They were known never to miss a Spring Island dove shoot and were great additions to any gathering.

Any guest who had shot their first Spring Island bird was ceremoniously presented with a silver pin bearing the island logo, a much-prized award. Then came time for everyone to wend his or her way back to the island dock and across the river. There, if desired, "one for the road" was available, and off they all went with memories of another great Spring Island day.

More treasured, perhaps, are memories of spur of the moment dove shooting when a few of us would sit at dawn or dusk, in the Tabby Ruins or the pecan orchard, waiting quietly for the doves to come in. The early morning mists or the setting sun made such moments magical, whether or not we shot any birds.

Another very special memory for me is the first time I rode a horse from St. Francis down the lane to the Tabby Ruins. You can ride in a car, walk, or bike, but nothing gives you the feeling of centuries past like being on horseback.

Sallie Mae Hollings, Cora Lee Bull, Helen Frances Stokes, 1982.

Opposite: Lucile Walker Hays at dove shoot.

Opposite: Lucile & Bill Hays (photo by Betsy Chaffin).

The Later Years

M Y FATHER DIED of a heart attack unexpectedly in March 1973 at the age of sixty-two. He had accomplished so much in only nine years and was enjoying this island to the fullest. I never had a chance to talk to him about his vision for the future of the island.

My mother continued on with her winter schedule and actually was on the island most of the year. She always brought her poodles down with her. In earlier years, they were gray miniatures, Grissette and Toto, and in later years, there was a chocolate named Beau.

My mother loved entertaining her guests and hunting. She kept meticulous records—four large photo albums and guest books for every island event.

Gordon was devoted to my mother and took very good care of her. I know she lived longer than she would have without his attention. Doc Jenkins always made sure that Gordon had whatever might be needed for emergencies and came out himself whenever appropriate. My mother was always the happiest when she was on Spring Island. She was sixty-eight when she died in 1982.

A highlight of those years was the marriage of my sister, Elaine, to George F. Fiske, Jr. in March 1977. It was the first wedding to be held at the St. Francis statue and was a great occasion. James B. Edwards, the governor of South Carolina at the time, officiated. The bride and groom were driven in style on their wedding day. The mules were dressed in white bonnets and ribbons for the occasion, and bells were strung behind the wagon.

My sister had a close friend by the name of Jane Sampson who was an excellent photographer. She took a series of pictures of the island—our house, the Tabby Ruins, and wildlife that are among the best that I have from the old days. I am happy to be able to include some in this book and have credited her with those that appear.

After 1982, our family ran the plantation as a business. As my sister had small children at that time, I spent a good deal of time on the island preparing for paying guests. The house needed redecorating, and we needed efficient household help.

I loved being at Spring Island more often, as our daughter, Kitty, was living in Beaufort at the time with her husband, Graham McBride. He taught at Beaufort Academy for four years and then at the Beaufort Marine Institute for two years. Our first

Elaine Walker Hoffman and Betsy, Bill, Kitty & Lucile Hays, 1975.

Opposite: St. Francis of Assisi statue (photograph by Jane Sampson).

Mules on their way to the wedding.

Waiting to carry the bride and groom away.

Elaine and George Fiske on their wedding day, March 19, 1977.

The bride and groom, Mr. & Mrs. George Fiske, leaving their wedding.

Overleaf: Tabby Ruins (photographs by Jane Sampson).

Living room of Walker House (photograph by Jane Sampson).

Dining room of Walker House (photograph by Jane Sampson).

grandchild, Elizabeth Anne McBride, was born in Beaufort Memorial Hospital on November 21,1986. Kitty and Graham were able to visit the island frequently and developed such a close relationship with Gordon that they asked him to be the baby's godfather.

Fay Anathan, a friend from Nantucket, accompanied me on one of those visits. On a dark and rainy night at about 9 P.M., we were sitting by the dying fire in our house, the "Walker House". Gordon had taken the cook, Flowers, across the river and had returned, and we were about to call it a day. The only other human being on the island was Gordon's daughter, Pete, who was asleep in her bed at his house.

Suddenly, someone hammered the brass knocker on the door, shattering our quiet evening, and we all jumped a mile into the air. I was so thankful Gordon was still there and I did not have to respond myself. Opening the door, Gordon saw a very wet and tired

man who said his boat had run out of gas and he had beached it near a round, glass building. This, of course, was the Gazebo. He had walked for an hour or more until he saw the lights of our house. He asked where the road was so he could hitchhike.

I felt sorry for the man, but Gordon gave him a very hard time. After grilling him thoroughly, Gordon let him call home and then took the poor fellow across the river.

We rented the island by the week during the quail season for four hunters and spouses or a total of eight people. The rentals were on the same schedule as my mother's guest schedule had been—arrival on Sunday afternoon, five days of hunting, and departure on Saturday morning. Up until that time, Gordon had always taken everyone out quail hunting himself. With the advent of rentals, he could not hunt all day

Opposite: Bill Hays and Gordon Mobley at fireplace.

Overleaf: Lucile Hays in mosquito veil with Jet; Bill Hays on Ebony.

and run the plantation, so he hired his brother Joe to be in charge of hunting. Gordon needed someone he could rely on because of the liability involved with paying guests. From then on, Joe Mobley and William Fripp ran the hunt, Marion Cooler drove the wagon, and James Mitchell assisted.

My husband, Bill, and I reserved one week in quail season for our own use, as did my sister, Elaine. We had some very special house parties during that time,

especially with our good friends the Whitcombs and the Millingtons. It was a magical time when we had the island to ourselves and could enjoy many special experiences in this remote island paradise.

George and Connie Trask were introduced to us by my mother's good friend Helen Frances Stokes, and she told us all we would like each other. We certainly did, and often enjoyed hunts and cookouts with the Trask family.

We spent two Christmases here with our daughters, Kitty and Betsy. What fun it was finding an island Christmas tree and sharing it all with Gordon and his family. One Christmas was so cold that pipes froze, and we had a frigid memorable hunt along the north shore of Pine Island; the second Christmas was eighty degrees, and we went fishing in shorts!

We had five hundred acres planted in soybeans and corn. Gordon and I even turned over one of the duck ponds to rice growing. I don't really think we believed we could make money on that. Gordon started farming shrimp; hence the name of The Shrimp Pond, hoping that would help the bottom line.

We also did selective timbering. I went with Gordon to Savannah to pick out a skidder, which we leased along with two timber trucks. Watching a timber truck leave the island was a nerve-wracking experience. The bow dipped under water when the full weight of the truck hit the barge; and when loaded, the freeboard was minimal.

Left: Lucile Hays and Clark Whitcomb.

*Opposite: Clark Whitcomb, Gordon Mobley, Lucile Hays,
Nancy Whitcomb, and William Fripp.*

*Overleaf: Lucile Hays and Gordon Mobley in rice field;
George Fiske and Bill Hays holding quail.*

The Tabby Ruins had not been attended to since the beginning when they were cleared out and the wires were put in to hold up the wall on the south side. We heard that Colin Brooker was the man to call to preserve them, and I called him in 1983. He put the frames in the windows and capped the tops of the walls to minimize disintegration of the tabby from wet weather.

After several years, it became apparent that we could not produce the revenue required to support the island. The sea wall and docks needed a great deal of work, and it was expensive keeping boats and a barge, trucks and cars on mainland and island. Therefore, after lengthy discussions and with deep regret, the decision was made to let Spring Island go. It was not easy to watch strangers touring the island and hear what they would do with it. I hosted a luncheon for an Arab sheik who visited with an eye to buying the island, but his eye fell on one of Gordon's daughters instead. He did not last long! We had one deal with a group that would have developed the island intensively, with a new village to be established down by the Gazebo. I am so glad that did not happen

John Carswell writes:

> After twenty years of many most enjoyable dove and quail hunts, Lucile and Elaine, and Mr. Adams, their trustee, decided to sell Spring Island and entered into a contract. We recipients of Walker hospitality and generosity during the twenty years were invited to one last shoot. Following the shoot, we presented Lucile Hays with twelve red roses and a box of Whitman chocolates, with much speaking, crying and hugging. Happily the deal with that buyer was not consummated, and the hunts continued! Chaffin, Light and LaMotte finally concluded a purchase, and thanks to the considerable courtesies of the Walkers and Gordon Mobley, Peggy and I were happy to continue our Spring Island association by buying a lot and building a house. The Walker legacy has continued through Lucile and Bill Hays' lot ownership, presence, and interest in the island. They could not have picked a better buyer than the talented, honest, resourceful, Christian group headed by Jim Chaffin, Jim Light, and Peter LaMotte.

I thank the Chaffins, Lights, and LaMottes for recognizing what an incredibly special island they had found. They have created a community that fits into nature, giving everyone the opportunity to appreciate much of the island the way it has always been. I hope that all the owners of the future will experience the peace and beauty that is still here and protect it for eternity.

Oyster shells in wall of Tabby Ruins (photograph by Jane Sampson).

Opposite: Lucile Hays sitting in the Gazebo.

116

Opposite: Lucile Hays and cook Lee Maulden picking vegetables for dinner.

Spring Island Plantation Recipes

MY MOTHER HAD various early cooks that I really do not remember. The one we had the longest, and right up until my mother's death, was named Flowers, who arrived wearing a new wig every day. She lived in Hardeeville and did not drive. Someone had to go get her and bring across the river every day in time to cook breakfast—and that was grits, eggs, bacon, toast, and more. She did not leave until after dinner, and remember that was by boat—what a long day. Flowers suffered from high blood pressure and oc-casionally would call in sick. Then Janice Mobley and her girls had to pinch hit in the kitchen. We did have a wonderful lady named Jessie who took care of the house, and she would help them. Jessie also provided us with fresh eggs from her chickens. We found a detailed description of how to set the table written out by Janice, which follows:

Serve Mrs. Walker first, and then the other ladies, then Mr. Walker next, and then the other men. Table setting: candles, salt and pepper, place mats, ash tray and matches, coaster for water glass (right

120

Kitty and Betsy Hays enjoying Spring Island oyster roast.

Opposite: Lucile and Bill Hays admiring their oyster roast at the Gazebo.

side above knife), appropriate knife, spoon on right side. Appropriate forks on left side. If bread will be served, place butter knife on bread and butter plate and place this above plate at left. Put service plate on mat. When ready to serve, place soup bowl and plate or salad bowl on service plate. After this course is finished, remove all this from right side. Place dinner plate on mat from left side. Serve meat first from left, then vegetables (one at a time) from left. After main course, remove all dishes and utensils from right. Place dessert plate (with fork and spoon on it) from left. Serve dessert from left. Put tray with coffee and cups and saucers on table in front of the sofa.

I can't believe it—they forgot the napkins!

In 1982, when we decided to rent out the plantation to hunting parties, we needed a more accomplished and reliable cook. Gordon asked around in Waynesboro and found a retired lady by the name of Lee Maulden. She had just turned over her restaurant to her son and thought she would take it easy. Gordon persuaded her otherwise, and she took our job. She told me she thought it would be fun to do something so totally different, and I think she loved being here. We turned over one of the little guesthouses to her, and sometimes she did not go home for a month or more.

When I first asked her what she liked to cook, her reply was grits and red-eyed gravy. I said that was fine but we needed a varied menu for the folks who would come from the North. My sister and I worked up a two-week menu, but gradually over the years it became adapted to Lee's cooking and her favorites.

Lee wrote a cookbook by hand for me. Many of the recipes included here come from her book; some are from the Flowers era; and the crab boil is from Donna Mobley Carter. Some recipes make me realize how much our taste in cooking has changed.

Lowcountry Feasts

Two dishes haven't changed for hundreds of years along the South Carolina coast; they were specialties at our Spring Island gatherings, and I will start with them:

Oyster Roast

Go down to creek and get bushel of oysters. Scrub thoroughly with cold water to remove mud from shells. Dig pit outside and get good fire going in it. Wait until fire burns down to coals; put 4 x 8-foot heavy-metal sheet over pit. Place oysters on top and cover with wet burlap. Let steam 15-20 minutes; oysters should open easily. Spread newspapers over 4 x 8-foot plywood sheet on sawhorses outside. Pour steaming oysters on newspapers. Have gloves and oyster knives ready along with melted butter and cocktail sauce. Serve with white wine and beer.

Crab Boil

Go down to creek and get bushel of crabs and 3-5 pounds shrimp. Shuck, wash, and break into halves 1 dozen ears fresh Silver Queen corn. Outside house, fill with fresh water to half capacity a 60-quart pot with a strainer and lid. Add half box Morton's salt. Cover with lid. Cook over high flame on outdoor propane burner until water comes to full rolling boil. Add 3 or more pounds of inch-long pieces of Hillshire smoked-beef sausage, 3 pounds of peeled, small yellow onions, and a handful of whole new potatoes. Bring back to boil for 10 minutes, longer if cocktail hour warrants. Gather all guests around pot to see crabs. Using huge shrimper's gloves (think

Oyster roast heaven: Nancy Whitcomb, Marion Cooler, Gordon Mobley, William Fripp, Lee Maulden, and Lucile Hays.

electrical lineman), carefully pour live crabs into boiling water. Stop when crabs reach water mark, leaving remainder for second cooking so guests have fresh hot crabs. From this moment on timing is very important; cook should stay close to pot. As soon as water comes back to rolling boil add corn. Cover and time for exactly 8 minutes. Have someone test a claw or two, mostly for effect. Add 3-5 pounds fresh, white shrimp. Cover and cook two more minutes. Again, test a couple of crabs just to be sure. Using protective mitts, carefully lift strainer from pot and let drain.

Cook must now call guests to gather around table thoroughly covered with old newspapers. Guests hold up edges of newspapers to prevent errant ingredients from rolling onto floor. Cook shakes strainer basket to scatter crabs, sausage, onions, corn, potatoes, and shrimp evenly over table. Guests sit around table and eat together right on the newspapers.

Serve crabs with cocktail sauce and hot melted butter. Use empty eight-ounce glass Coca-Cola bottles or handle end of table knives as hammer to crack open claws. When everyone has had his fill, clean up is a simple process. Roll newspaper, crab shells, and all towards middle of table, creating large ball. Slide rolled ball into a 39-gallon lawn-and-leaf trash bag. Guests will be amazed once more.

Cocktail Sauce

1 bottle Heinz chili sauce
Juice from 1 lemon
2 tablespoons fresh horseradish sauce
1 tablespoon Worcestershire sauce
salt & pepper to taste
Mix well, serve in individual dishes.
Donna Mobley Carter

Appetizers and Soups

Crab Balls

½ cup cooked crab or 1 can
3 ounces cream cheese
½ teaspoon salt
1 teaspoon lemon juice
½ teaspoon celery seed
Dash of pepper
Pretzel sticks
Blend all ingredients together, mixing thoroughly. Chill. Form into bite size balls. Keep well chilled until party time, then stick a thin, two-inch pretzel stick into each ball for a small handle. Makes 25.

Hot Crab Dip

1 eight-ounce package cream cheese, softened
¼ cup grated Parmesan cheese
¼ cup thinly sliced scallions
¼ cup mayonnaise
¼ cup dry white wine
2 teaspoons sugar
1 teaspoon ground mustard (dry)
1 clove garlic, finely chopped
1 six-ounce can crabmeat, drained and flaked
½ cup toasted, sliced almonds
Preheat oven to 375.
Mix all ingredients except crabmeat and almonds in a bowl until well blended. Stir in crab. Spread crab mixture in shallow, one-quart casserole. Sprinkle with almonds. Bake uncovered 15 to 20 minutes or until hot and bubbly. Serve with crackers.

More oyster roast heaven: Clark & Nancy Whitcomb, Marion Cooler, John Millington, and William Fripp.

Cheese Toast Rounds

½ stick butter
½ pound New York extra sharp Cheddar cheese, grated
2 tablespoons mayonnaise
2 tablespoons Dijon mustard
Toast bread, then cut in rounds. Mix well. Mound on toasted rounds and place under broiler for five minutes. Sprinkle cayenne pepper on top.

Cheese Cookies

½ cup butter
½ pound New York extra sharp Cheddar cheese, grated
1 cup flour
½ teaspoon salt
¼ teaspoon cayenne pepper
2 teaspoons onion soup mix
½ cup pecans to garnish
Mix butter and cheese together well; add rest of ingredients. Roll dough on floured board and cut with small cutter. Bake at 350 degrees for 20 to 25 minutes. Makes 6 dozen

Spinach and Artichoke Dip

1 can (14 ounces) artichoke hearts, drained and chopped
1 package (10 ounces) frozen, chopped spinach, thawed and drained
1 cup mayonnaise (regular or light)
1½ cups grated Parmesan cheese (I like to use half Parmesan and half Romano)
2 cups shredded Monterey Jack cheese

2 teaspoons Worcestershire sauce
Preheat oven to 350. Lightly grease a one-quart baking dish.
In a medium bowl, mix together artichoke hearts, spinach, mayonnaise, a cup of the Parmesan, Monterey Jack, and Worcestershire. Transfer to baking dish and sprinkle top with remaining Parmesan. Bake in the center of the oven until cheese is bubbling, about 30 minutes.
Prepare this dish ahead, but serve it warm from the oven with fresh bread, crackers, chips, etc. Prep time is approximately 10 minutes. Cook time is 30 to 40 minutes.
Makes 3 cups.

Spinach Dip

1 package frozen, chopped spinach, drained
1 package Knorr vegetable soup mix
1 can water chestnuts, drained
16 ounces sour cream
Mix in food processor. Serve with raw vegetables.

Oyster Crackers

1 package Hidden Valley Ranch Italian dressing mix
¼ teaspoon lemon pepper
½ teaspoon dill weed
¼ teaspoon garlic powder
¾ cup olive oil
1 package plain oyster crackers
Mix first five ingredients well, then mix with oyster crackers. Spread in baking pan and bake at 325 for 15 minutes.
Miss Lee: "These are nice to have on hand for friends who drop in!"

Gordon Mobley pouring a bushel of Atlantic blue crabs into the boiling pot.

"Sandwich"

1 egg
¾ cup sugar
¾ cup mayonnaise
1 cup raisins
1 cup chopped pecans
Juice of one lemon
Beat the egg; add sugar. Cook in double boiler slowly for several minutes. Add raisins and cook until puffy. Add mayo, nuts, and lemon juice.
(Dear Reader, what would you do with this?)

Grandma Rathbun's Bread and Butter Pickles

6 quarts of cucumbers, sliced thin
1 quart of sliced onions
4 large green peppers, chopped fine. Let vegetables stand in brine overnight (one cup salt to 9 cups water). Drain well in morning and add:
6 cups mild vinegar
1 teaspoon white celery seed
1 teaspoon mustard seed
1 tablespoon turmeric
Bring to boiling point, but do NOT boil. Seal hot.

Zucchini or Asparagus Soup

1 pound zucchini or asparagus
1 small onion, quartered
1 cup chicken broth
1 teaspoon salt
¼ teaspoon pepper
½ teaspoon sweet basil
Chop zucchini and put everything in a pot. Simmer 20 minutes. Blend at high speed in blender. Stock may be frozen at this point.
To serve, add 1½ cups milk and ½ cup cream. This is good hot or cold.

Cold Cucumber Soup

1 medium onion, chopped
1 medium cucumber, peeled and cubed
¾ cup chicken broth
1 can cream of chicken soup
1 cup sour cream
6 dashes of Tabasco
6 dashes of Worcestershire
¼ teaspoon celery salt
¼ teaspoon curry
Blend all the above at high speed in blender and serve.

Lunch and Dinner Dishes

Tuna Chowder

1 can white tuna in oil
2 medium onions
1 pound fatback
1 can mushroom soup
1 can cream of potato soup
1 can milk
4 tablespoons sherry
Fry out the fatback, place on paper towels. Sauté onions in drippings. Mix all other ingredients and heat to simmer. Serve with a tablespoon of crumbled fatback sprinkled on each bowl.

Gordon and SaSa Mobley pour crab boil straight from the pot onto newspapers.

Crabmeat Casserole

3 cans or 1 pound fresh crabmeat
4 tablespoons butter
3 tablespoons flour
¼ teaspoon each of salt and pepper
Paprika
½ pound mushrooms
1¼ cups of milk
1 ounce grated Cheddar cheese
1½ ounces sherry

Sauté mushrooms in 2 tablespoons of butter, blend in flour, salt and pepper. Add milk and stir until thick. Add cheese and stir, then add mushrooms and crabmeat. Add sherry.

Butter casserole, fill with mixture, sprinkle with breadcrumbs, and dot with remaining butter. Bake at 350 until bubbly and serve with rice.

Grilled Shrimp

2 pounds shrimp in shells
1 cup salad oil
1 cup freshly squeezed lemon juice
2 teaspoons Italian dressing mixture
2 teaspoons seasoned salt
1 teaspoon seasoned pepper
4 tablespoons brown sugar
2 tablespoons soy sauce
½ cup chopped green onion

Shell and wash shrimp. Drain on paper towels. Mix all ingredients together and marinate shrimp. Put shrimp on skewers and grill. Boil marinade and use for sauce.

Lee's Shrimp Creole

4 tablespoons bacon drippings
2 medium onions
1 green pepper
1½ cups celery
1 quart canned tomatoes
3 teaspoons sugar
3 tablespoons tomato paste
Salt and pepper to taste
3 cups cooked shrimp

Cut up onions, pepper, and celery, sauté in bacon drippings. Add tomatoes, sugar, and tomato paste. Let this mixture simmer slowly to thicken for about 30 minutes. Add salt and pepper to taste. Five minutes before serving, add shrimp and heat thoroughly.

Lucile's Shrimp Creole

2 tablespoons olive oil
2 cups white onions, sliced
4 cloves garlic, sliced
4 celery ribs, diced
2 medium green peppers, seeded and diced
½ teaspoon cayenne pepper
2 to 3 cans seasoned, cooked, chopped tomatoes
1 can tomato paste
2 bay leaves
1 teaspoon dried thyme or Italian herbs
2 pounds shelled, raw shrimp
1 teaspoon Old Bay seasoning

In large pot or wok, heat oil. Add onions and cook 1 minute. Add garlic and cook 30 seconds. Add celery, peppers, Old Bay, and cayenne. Reduce heat to medium and cook 2 to 3 minutes. Add tomatoes and herbs. Simmer 15 minutes, stir in paste. Simmer

Crab boil heaven.

until thickened. You can do this ahead. Just before eating, bring mixture back to a simmer, add shrimp, and stir until they are cooked—5 to 8 minutes. Sprinkle with cilantro or parsley. Serve with white or brown rice.

Veal Marsala

4 veal scallops, pounded thin
Salt
Freshly ground pepper
4 tablespoons butter
1 clove garlic, crushed
½ pound of mushrooms, sliced
½ cup good Marsala wine
Melt 3 tablespoons butter in skillet. Sauté garlic until golden brown. Add veal and brown well on both sides. Transfer to heavy, shallow baking pan. Add remaining tablespoon butter to skillet and sauté mushrooms 2 or 3 minutes. Add wine and simmer 2 minutes. Pour over veal in baking dish and bake covered at 350 degrees for 15 minutes.

Chicken Stir-Fry

1 can (15 ounces) pineapple chunks in juice; drain and reserve ½ cup of juice for sauce
1 tablespoon cornstarch
3 tablespoons vinegar
1 tablespoon honey
2 tablespoons olive oil
1 pound boneless, skinless chicken breasts, cut into ¾-inch pieces
1 medium bell pepper, cut into ¾-inch pieces
1 medium onion, sliced
2 medium carrots, coarsely shredded

Mix reserved pineapple juice, cornstarch, vinegar, and honey. Heat wok or 12-inch skillet over high heat. Add 1 tablespoon of oil and rotate wok to coat sides. Add chicken. Stir-fry about 4 minutes or until chicken is no longer pink in the center. Remove and keep warm. Add 1 tablespoon of oil to wok and coat sides. Add pepper and onion and stir-fry one minute. Add cornstarch mixture and carrots to wok. Cook and stir about 1 minute until sauce thickens. Stir in pineapple and chicken and heat thoroughly.
Lee added this note: "I use this for shrimp as we don't get shrimp that often. Ha ha!"

Red Rice

2 strips of bacon
1 cup raw rice (Uncle Ben's)
1 cup tomato juice
1 cup strong bouillon
1 small onion, chopped
Salt and pepper
Cook bacon until crisp. Sauté onion in drippings, but do not brown. Remove to baking dish. Add and mix remaining ingredients, cover tightly, and bake at 350 degrees for 1 hour.
Donna's note: This is best cooked in cast iron.

Brown Rice

1½ cups brown rice
1 can beef broth
1½ cups water
1 teaspoon Italian or French herbs
½ lb. mushrooms sautéed in 1 tablespoon olive oil
Put all ingredients in covered baking dish , dot with butter, and bake for an hour at 350 degrees.

Bill Hays, Gordon Mobley, SaSa Mobley, Clark Whitcomb, and Nancy Whitcomb in crab boil heaven.

Cheese Grits Soufflé

5 tablespoons butter
¼ cup onions, finely chopped
2 cups water
½ teaspoon salt
½ cup quick grits
1 teaspoon Tabasco
Freshly ground black pepper
1¾ cups Cheddar cheese, grated
3 tablespoons butter, softened
2 egg whites
Melt 2 tablespoons butter and add onions. Cook about 4 minutes. Do not brown. Boil 2 cups water. Add salt, and pour grits in slowly. Boil about 1 minute, stirring constantly. Then reduce heat and cook another 2 minutes. Add onions, Tabasco, a few grinds of black pepper, 1½ cups of the grated cheese, and remaining butter and mix well. Lightly butter casserole dish. Beat egg whites until stiff peaks form. Thoroughly fold egg whites into grits mixture. Pour into casserole and sprinkle top with remaining cheese. Bake at 400 degrees for 30 minutes or until puffed and lightly browned. Serves 4.

Carrot Soufflé

2 cups carrots, cooked and mashed
½ cup butter, softened
¾ cup sugar
¼ teaspoon cinnamon
1 tablespoon flour
1 teaspoon baking powder
1 teaspoon salt
1 cup milk
Beat all ingredients together in food processor. Put in dish and bake 45 minutes at 350 degrees.

Salads

Broccoli Salad

1 bunch of broccoli (use only buds, chopped fine)
¼ cup chopped onion
½ cup chopped red bell pepper
¼ cup chopped pecans
4 hard-boiled eggs, chopped
Salt and pepper
Dressing:
1 cup mayonnaise
2 tablespoons Dijon mustard
2 tablespoons lemon juice
Mix all ingredients together and let stand overnight.

Curried Chicken Salad

2 chicken breasts, poached and cut into chunks
1 can water chestnuts
¼ cup toasted almonds
½ cup seedless grapes, cut in half

Dressing:
½ cup mayonnaise
½ cup nonfat yogurt
2 tablespoons curry powder
Prepare curry powder by heating it with 2 tablespoons oil over low heat for 30 seconds or until you start to smell the curry. Cool and then add to mayo and yogurt. Add to chicken mixture. Serve over lettuce.

Donna Mobley serving Edwina Millington and Clark Whitcomb.

Game

The duck press used to live on one end of a long, low sideboard in the dining room of our house on Long Island. On the other end, there was a chafing dish. My father loved to go duck hunting at the Southside Club on Shelter Island, and cooking the duck was a major production. This is a French specialty made famous by La Tour d'Argent in Paris. First, wild duck has to be cooked just right—rare. The breast meat and the legs are carefully carved off the bone and laid on a platter. Then the carcass is put in the cylinder of the duck press. The big wheel on top is turned, pressing a plate down on the carcass. This extracts all the juices, which run out the spout at the base of the press. Then my father would make the gravy in the chafing dish using the juice mixed with butter, reduced red wine, foie gras, and cognac. It certainly was a gourmet meal!

Donna's Game Birds

12 quail or dove, picked and dressed
¼ cup butter
¼ cup olive oil
4-5 strips bacon
2-3 tablespoons all-purpose flour
½ medium onion, chopped
8 ounces mushrooms
2 cups chicken broth (or 1 can)
½ cup white wine
½ cup Mr. & Mrs. T. Bloody Mary Mix

Cooked Rice

Melt butter with oil in a large skillet over medium high heat. Lightly flour and season birds with salt and pepper. Brown birds, breast side down first. Remove birds from skillet, arrange in casserole, and set aside. Sauté onions and mushrooms, spread over birds. Lay bacon slices over the top. Brown 2 tablespoons flour in remaining butter/oil (add a little more if necessary) and scrape up brown bits. Stir in chicken broth, add Bloody Mary mix and wine, and cook until the mixture starts to thicken. Pour over the birds in casserole. Bake covered 45 minutes at 350 degrees. Raise heat to 425 and cook 15 minutes uncovered.
Donna Mobley Carter

Left: Duck press.

Opposite: Gordon Mobley cooking quail at the Gazebo.

Gordon's BBQ Quail

Melt about a stick of butter for 6 quail. Add a table-spoon *Herbes de Provence* from Hediard in Paris. Drop each quail in pot to coat thoroughly with butter mixture. Grill until done. Serve with red rice.

Englishmen's Quail

This is the recipe the Englishmen gave to Lee Maulden which she cooked for them when they were down at Spring Island:

Salt and pepper the quail and fry, turning. Remove from pan and put in warm oven. Add red wine, water, salt and pepper, a pint of cream, red current jelly, gravy browning, and a little blue cheese. Cook down. Heat birds in sauce for a few minutes and serve with wild rice.

Spring Island Venison Steaks

4 venison steaks
Worcestershire sauce
3 tablespoons butter
½ pound mushrooms, sliced
1 medium onion
Salt and pepper
Accent
Blackened seasoning
Marinate venison in Worcestershire sauce for an hour. Sauté onions and mushrooms in butter until tender. Remove from pan and keep warm. Season both sides of venison steaks with Accent and seasonings. Sauté a few minutes on each side until the steaks reach desired doneness. Serve with onion/mushroom mixture on top.

Mr. Hadley's Duck

Wash and dry duck inside and out. Chop onion, apple, and celery, put in cavity. Rub bacon grease all over. Sprinkle well with celery salt. Bake in oven at 500 degrees uncovered 20 to 25 minutes, or bake them on a hot grill. Make sure you use ducks that were plucked and still have their skin.

Mrs. Hadley's Dove

Eight dove washed and dried inside and out. Combine in a bag and mix well ¼ cup flour, one teaspoon salt, and 12 teaspoons pepper. Flour two birds at a time. Hit birds on bag to remove excess flour. Heat a pan and put in ¼ stick of butter. Drop birds in heated butter, breasts down, and brown well, then add ¼ cup of red wine, ¼ cup water, and two bay leaves. Cover pan, reduce heat, and simmer birds for about 15 minutes or until tender, turning frequently.

John and Lucille Hadley.

138

Quail roasting on the grill (photograph by Jane Sampson).

Sauce for Game Birds

Dove: ½ stick butter, 2 tablespoons cranberry jelly, 1 ounce port wine. Melt butter and jelly, add wine.

Quail: Substitute currant jelly for the cranberry.

Roseanne Beard's Quail

Split quail; wash and dry. Lay birds flat on pan. Put small strips of bacon on top. Preheat oven, cook quail 20 minutes at 400 degrees.

Breads

Cheesy Mexican Corn Bread

1½ cups yellow or white cornmeal
½ cup all purpose flour
1 cup buttermilk
¼ cup vegetable oil
2 teaspoons baking powder
¼ cup sugar
2 teaspoons salt
½ teaspoon baking soda
2 large eggs
1 eight-ounce can corn
1 four-ounce can chopped green chilies, well drained (can use hot ones)
½ cup shredded Monterey Jack or sharp Cheddar (two ounces)
2 teaspoons chili powder

Heat oven to 450 degrees. Grease bottom and sides of round pan. (I use my 9-inch iron fry pan.) Mix all ingredients. Beat vigorously 30 seconds. Pour batter into pan. Bake 25 to 30 minutes until golden brown. Serve warm.

Spiced Bran Muffins

Vegetable oil cooking spray
½ cup molasses
2 tablespoons honey
2 large egg whites
¼ cup plain nonfat yogurt
¼ cup milk
½ cup wheat bran
1 cup whole wheat flour
1½ teaspoons baking powder
1 tablespoon ground ginger
1 teaspoon ground cloves
¼ cup chopped walnuts
¼ cup raisins

Preheat oven to 350 degrees. Coat a 12-cup muffin tin with cooking spray. Warm the molasses and honey in a small saucepan over low heat just until it begins to steam. Remove the pan from the heat and set aside to cool. Whisk the egg whites, yogurt, and milk together in a large mixing bowl until blended. Whisk in the molasses/honey mixture. Using a wooden spoon, stir in the bran, flour, baking powder, and spices. Fold in walnuts and raisins. Bake 15 to 20 minutes until toothpick inserted into center of a muffin comes out clean. Serve warm.

Author's note: This recipe was mailed to me in Nantucket with the following lovely note from Lee: "I know you will like these as they are so good. Wish I was there to make them for you all!"

Lucile Hays, Gordon Mobley, and George & Connie Trask wait for the quail to cook.

Bran Date Muffins

½ cup hot water
¼ cup chopped dates
1½ cups wheat bran
1 cup whole wheat flour
1 teaspoon baking powder
½ teaspoon baking soda
½ teaspoon salt
⅓ cup vegetable oil
1 egg
1 cup buttermilk
½ cup chopped dates

Pour water over ¼ cup dates and set aside. Heat oven to 400 degrees. Grease bottom only of 12 medium muffin cups or line with paper baking cups. Mix wheat bran, flour, baking powder, soda, and salt in large bowl. Place date water mixture, oil, and egg in blender or food processor. Cover and blend until smooth. Combine date mixture, flour mixture, and buttermilk just until flour is moistened. (Batter will be lumpy.) Gently stir in ½ cup dates. Divide batter evenly among muffin cups. Bake 20 to 25 minutes or until toothpick inserted in center comes out clean. Cool in pan 5 minutes, then remove to wire rack.

Lemon Oat Scones

⅓ cup cold butter
1¼ cups all purpose flour
½ cup quick cooking oats
3 tablespoons sugar
2½ teaspoons baking powder
2 teaspoons grated lemon peel
¼ teaspoon salt
1 large egg, beaten
½ cup raisins or currants
4 to 6 tablespoons light cream or half and half
1 large egg beaten

Cut butter into flour, oats, sugar, baking powder, lemon peel, and salt in medium bowl using pastry blender or crisscrossing two knives until mixture looks like fine crumbs. Stir in egg, raisins, and just enough cream so dough leaves side of bowl. Turn dough onto lightly floured surface. Knead lightly 10 times. Roll or pat to ½-inch thick. Cut into diamond shapes with sharp knife. Place on ungreased cookie sheet. Brush dough with beaten egg. Bake 10 to 12 minutes or until golden brown. Remove to wire rack. Serve warm.

Angel Buns

1 package quick-acting active dry yeast
1 tablespoon sugar
¼ cup warm water, 105 to 115 degrees
2 cups original Bisquick
¼ cup milk

Dissolve yeast and sugar in warm water in medium bowl. Mix in baking mix and milk until dough forms. Gently smooth into ball on surface dusted with baking mix. Knead 10 times and roll out to 1-inch thick. Cut with 2-inch biscuit cutter. Place on ungreased cookie sheet. Let rise in warm place about 30 minutes. Heat oven to 425 degrees. Bake 6 to 8 minutes until golden brown.

Desserts

Oatmeal Raisin Cookies

1¼ cups butter
¾ cup firmly packed brown sugar
½ cup white sugar
1 egg
1 teaspoon vanilla
1½ cups plain flour
1 teaspoon baking soda
1 teaspoon salt
1 teaspoon cinnamon
1 cup pecans or walnuts
1 cup raisins
3 cups Quaker oats
Heat oven to 375 degrees. Beat together butter and sugar until light and fluffy. Beat in egg and vanilla. Combine flour, baking soda, salt, and cinnamon. Add to butter mixture and mix well. Stir in oats, raisins, and nuts. Drop on cookie sheet and cook 8 to 10 minutes for a chewy cookie, 10 to 11 minutes for a crisp cookie.
Note from Donna Carter: "Mrs. Lee used to hide these cookies at night so there would be some left for lunch the next day. She was afraid of midnight snackers!"

Apple Bars

1 cup packed brown sugar
¼ cup vegetable oil
¼ cup milk
1 large egg
2 cups all purpose flour
1 teaspoon baking soda
1 teaspoon ground cinnamon
½ teaspoon ground nutmeg
¼ teaspoon ground cloves
1½ cups peeled, cooked, chopped apples (two small)
1 cup chopped walnuts
Heat oven to 350 degrees. Grease bottom and sides of rectangular pan with shortening. Mix brown sugar, oil, milk, and egg in large bowl. Stir in flour, baking soda, cinnamon, nutmeg, and cloves. Stir in apples and walnuts and spread in pan. Bake about 20 minutes or until toothpick inserted in the center comes out clean. Cool 30 minutes. Drizzle with spice glaze.

Spice Glaze:

Mix ¾ cup powdered sugar, ¼ teaspoon ground cinnamon, 1 to 2 teaspoons apple juice or milk until smooth and spreadable.

Lemon Soufflé

1 envelope plain gelatin
¼ cup cold water
4 eggs, separated
1 cup sugar
½ teaspoon salt
2 teaspoons grated lemon rind
½ cup lemon juice
1 cup heavy cream, whipped
Sprinkle gelatin over water to soften. Put lemon juice, egg yolks, sugar, and salt in the top of a double boiler. Cook until thick. Stir in gelatin and 1 teaspoon lemon rind. Cool. Beat egg whites and fold into mixture. Fold in whipped cream. Sprinkle with lemon rind. Chill and serve.

Lee's Never Fail Pound Cake

½ pound butter, softened
3 cups sugar
6 eggs, added to mixture one at a time
3 cups plain flour
1 teaspoon each orange and lemon flavorings
½ pint whipping cream
Mix well. Bake at 350 degrees for 1½ hours.

Chocolate Crackle Sauce

2 tablespoons butter
½ cup finely chopped pecans
4 squares semisweet chocolate
Melt butter, then add nuts. Sauté until golden brown.
Remove from heat. Stir in chocolate until melted
and smooth. Serve warm.

Regal Chocolate Sauce

2 squares Baker's unsweetened chocolate
6 tablespoons water
½ cup sugar
Dash salt
3 tablespoons butter
¼ teaspoon vanilla
Melt chocolate with water and add sugar and salt.
Boil 2 to 3 minutes. Remove from heat. Stir in butter and vanilla.

Coffee Jelly

4 teaspoons gelatin (package is 2½ teaspoons)
⅓ cup brandy
3 cups hot coffee (make liquid equal that called for
on gelatin pack)
½ cup sugar
Dissolve gelatin with brandy. Stir in hot coffee and
sugar. Stir well. Pour into cold (rinsed with cold
water) mold and chill. Serve with whipped cream.

Easy Chocolate Pots de Crème

1 package Nestle chocolate bits
2 eggs
⅓ cup milk
1 tablespoon sugar
1 tablespoon instant coffee
Dash of vanilla
Heat milk, sugar, coffee, and vanilla until simmer-
ing. Pour on top of chocolate bits and eggs in blender.
Blend until smooth and pour into pots. Refrigerate
for 8 hours.

Molded Raspberry Jelly

1 package frozen raspberries
1 package raspberry gelatin
½ cup water
½ cup boiling water
1 tablespoon lemon juice
⅓ cup evaporated milk

Thaw and drain berries, reserve juice. Soften gelatin in ½ cup water, add boiling water and stir. Add raspberry juice and lemon juice. Stir in milk and beat 5 to 10 minutes until mixture is fluffy and forms peaks. Fold in berries. Pour into quart mold or individual molds and chill. Serve with whipped cream. Serves 4 to 6.

To make jellies unmold easily, coat lightly inside with vegetable oil and let stand full of cold water while you mix ingredients.

Pecan Fudge

1 package chocolate bits (12 ounces)
1 tablespoon butter
1 teaspoon vanilla
Dash salt
1 cup broken pecans

Melt chocolate in top of double boiler. Add and mix well the remaining ingredients. Drop by teaspoonfuls on waxed paper on cookie sheet. Refrigerate. Do *not* freeze.

Elisha Walker cutting his birthday cake, March 6, 1967.

145

Reminiscences

WHEN I FIRST thought about writing this book, I realized that all the people who had been here over the years were a large part of our Spring Island story. I therefore wrote to family and friends and asked for any stories they would like to write about their visits to Spring Island. What follows are all the wonderful memories that have been shared with me. They are a tribute to a great era in Spring Island's history.

D. Nelson Adams
New York, New York

Because of my long and close relationship with Elisha Walker, Jr., I have been asked to record my recollections of Spring Island after it passed into Elisha's hands. But first a word about that long relationship.

Elisha and I first came to know each other when we were classmates at the Buckley School in New York City. I think at that point we were about six years of age. We were not only classmates but immediately became good friends. That continued until we graduated and went to different boarding schools. It wasn't until we found ourselves in the same class at Yale College that our paths joined together again. I saw a lot of Elisha during my four years at Yale, and we had a great deal of fun together.

After graduation, Elisha went into banking and subsequently gravitated into oil and gas exploration. I attended law school and thereafter was employed by the office of Davis, Polk and Wardwell, later becoming a partner. In the course of an oil and gas venture, Elisha became involved in some litigation with one of the participants and brought the case to me. I was fortunate to be able to settle the case on terms very satisfactory to Elisha, after which he brought all of his legal work to our office.

So it is not surprising that when Elisha called to tell me that he had purchased Spring Island, he was as excited as a young boy with an electric train at Christmas. He said he was going to establish a hunting preserve on the island, and he wanted to do it right because it would be combined with farming. Farming would provide feed for the birds and some open areas in strategic locations. Timbering would produce revenue. He figured he could use any losses the farm might incur for tax purposes. Very soon after that call, Elisha gathered up his accountants and myself for a visit to Spring Island.

Sometime later he hired a very young Gordon Mobley to manage the island and could not have made a better choice. Gordon knew hunting and he knew farming, and most of all, he had a winning way with people. I went down to the island with Elisha from time to time, but was not invited to participate in the hunting parties since it was well known that I could not hit my hat with a shotgun!

I do remember on those visits being met by Gordon at the Savannah Airport in the car that was permanently left on the mainland. Driven to the mainland dock, we were transferred with luggage to the motorboat, which Gordon would maneuver with unerring skill, no matter how dark the night. Upon arrival at the island dock, we were transferred to the car, which took us the short distance to the lodge. It always gave me a distinct thrill of anticipation when I stepped off the boat onto Spring Island. Once at the lodge, we changed to more casual clothing and, if the time of day made it appropriate, gathered in the living room and enjoyed some drinks in front of a roaring fire until it was time for dinner—usually

Gordon Mobley, Bill & Lucile Hays, and Nelson Adams.

an excellent steak prepared by the highly efficient and friendly staff.

Lucile and Elisha were apt to have guests from around the state—rather distinguished people. Louis Walker's roommate from his days at Yale was often invited, a lawyer from Charleston named Henry Smythe. I was told that Governor Jim Edwards had also visited, but I was not present when he came.

Before commencing the morning activities, we were treated to a large breakfast of hominy grits (an acquired taste), eggs and bacon, English muffins, with coffee or tea.

Then we walked over to the skeet field. Among the guests one morning was a former national skeet champion named Harold Floyd. He surveyed my dismal efforts and gave me a very helpful suggestion. He said, "As soon as the clay pigeon is released, lock the barrel of your gun on the target. Then move the barrel about two feet in front of the target while releasing the trigger. Keep moving the gun ahead after you feel the trigger has been released." It worked, but unfortunately I haven't had an opportunity to shoot any skeet since.

Among Elisha's most innovative ideas was the Gazebo, with its cigar store Indians and the magnificent statue of St. Francis gazing down through the beautiful lane of live oaks leading to the Tabby Ruins in the distance. There is no question about it: Whatever Elisha did, he did first class. In the area near the lodge, he also constructed the skeet range, a beautiful swimming pool, a tennis court, and a pitch and putt golf course. There were no tennis players among our generation, but on warm days, the pool got plenty of attention. I never saw anyone on the pitch and putt course—to my regret, since I had suggested it to Elisha.

Walks along the trails were absolutely beautiful as, of course, were tours of the island. I recall one lovely morning starting out from the lodge to inspect what had been accomplished since our previous visit. The lodge was beautifully situated on the river. To start on our way, we went out the drive that connected with the lane where if you turned left you went by Gordon's house, the big barn and paddocks, and down to the dock, whereas if you turned to the right, it led to the trails that wound their way around the island. The lane was, therefore, a rather key artery.

The area in the vicinity was relatively open with little in the way of vegetation except around the lodge itself. As we joined the lane, I heard Elisha say to Gordon, "You know, Gordon, it would be beautiful if we lined the sides of this road with live oaks."

That comment made an impression on me because I'm very fond of trees myself and have planted thousands in upstate New York. This was, incidentally, Elisha's courteous way of giving an order. The next time I visited the island, I noticed that young saplings had been evenly spaced along both sides of the lane, which had an immediate and attractive effect on the whole area. In future years I had the pleasure of seeing these young trees grow into sturdy oaks, and I wished them well on their long way to maturity. I can easily imagine what Elisha's oaks must look like today, marching majestically along the lane.

Lunch was usually served at the lodge, with grilled quail, wild rice, and salad on the menu. In the after-

noon, Lucile would try to corral any bridge players available and, if she succeeded, the card table was busy for the remainder of the afternoon. Dinner most likely would be cooked at the Gazebo with Gordon in charge. Steamed oysters and a big crab boil with shrimp and corn on the cob—we did not starve!

Eventually our idyllic visit had to come to an end. With departure imminent, we retraced our passage to the dock and boarded the boat to the mainland, looking back wistfully at Spring Island.

I will treasure the memories of my visits to Spring Island, memories of warm, congenial hosts, interesting guests, the lovely view from St. Francis down the lane of live oaks with the Tabby Ruins in the distance, the Gazebo with the rivers surrounding it (well almost), its wonderful views, and the parties we enjoyed there. And how could anyone forget the aroma of Gordon's cookouts—the oysters, the shrimp, the broiled quail—and the beauty of the woodlands, ponds, and meadows all combining to make Spring Island the extraordinary place that it is?

At my age I don't expect to see Spring Island again, but I read the reports and newsletters with avid interest and commend most highly the efforts that have been made to preserve and, yes, in some respects, to enhance this special piece of nature that God created.

Elisha died in 1973. His death closed a chapter on what had been really a remarkable regime. Elisha was an innovator and a born landscape artist. He left the island more beautiful, more accessible, more interesting, and more enjoyable than when he found it.

I consider myself most fortunate to have experienced the joys of Spring Island during this period in its wonderful history.

Kitty (Katharine) McBride holding her baby daughter, Zibby (Elizabeth) at Tabby Ruins.

Katharine Hays McBride
Orange, Virginia

When Mom asked me to write a piece for her book on Spring Island, I was flattered and believed it to be an easy task. I soon discovered that the more I tried to sort out the memories, the more came back to me. How can someone describe something that, on the one hand, is tangible, touching all five senses simultaneously, and on the other, is elusive and goes directly to your soul? What is Spring Island to me?

It is a place of sight: The painted buntings like little round rainbows eating at the birdfeeder outside the dining room of the house against the backdrop of the sea gray swaying Spanish moss. The black squirrels bounding like perfectly groomed kittens along the shrubs around the pool. The fiddler crabs at low tide, bumping and battling for their share in the formations that many a Parris Island drill instructor would appreciate.

It is a place of sound: The fronds of the palmettos scraping and sliding against each other. The early

151

morning rising of the birds, which depending on the person, is a lulling or a cacophony of arguing fishwives. The cry of "daaaiiyyd" as the dogs look for the fallen prey. The horses and mules work their bits, restless to move on. The sounds of the wagon; the jangling of the mules' bridles and the slish, slosh, rattle, crash of ice and drinks rolling, rocking, and swaying in counter time to the hoof beats. The sudden roar of a jet engine causes everyone to duck as the mighty Marine Corps fighter scrapes the tops of the trees.

It is a place of taste: The drinking water always had its own character, which like the island itself, one liked or not. Miss Jessie's breakfast, somehow impossible to recreate at home. (Maybe one had to fuss at the ingredients as she did.) Gordon's crab boils, whether done at the house, his house, or the Gazebo were the most elegantly barbaric feasts one could hope to have the honor to share.

It is a place of touch: The breeze rolling over the marsh and gently coaxing "the no-see-ems" off to find other prey. The Spanish moss, appearing deceptively soft but rough and alien when held. The exquisite itch of the chiggers as they gleefully feed on us who are silly enough to pick up and hold the Spanish moss. By the way, does anyone have any clear nail polish? The soft feathers of a dove or quail representing a successful hunt, but downy sadness all the same.

It is a place of smell: The marsh was the essence of Spring Island—sweet and sour, alluring and repelling, the smell of new life and death, of existence.

The island was a place both safe and dangerous. Dangerous for the foolhardy, who would think to wander at night and would enter the domain of the gator and snake. Stealthy, quiet, and ready for a meal,

they would be sure to provide an unforgettable if unrepeatable Spring Island experience.

Safe because either my family or Gordon was always there. The house was warm and full of laughter. Walking with my baby daughter, I would watch her learn about nature and quiet. St. Francis and the Tabby Ruins were places of reflection and daydreams of horse and buggies, hoops and crinoline dresses, top hats and duels for this or that person's honor. The mist carries the ghosts of the Edwards and their slaves. One could create such amazing stories if only one allowed the breeze, the moss, and the marsh to speak.

The Walker sisters, Lucile and Elaine, in 1975.

Kitty & Graham McBride.

Elizabeth Hays Carroll
Southborough, Massachusetts

For a young girl growing up in the heart of Manhattan, Spring Island was paradise. I was always excited to have the chance to spend my school vacations there. It was an all-day event just to get to the island from New York, and our journey would often culminate in a frantic dash from the car to the boat, as we had to race the tide. As the *Gobbler* made its way across the river, my anticipation and excitement would grow the closer we got. I could hardly wait to kick off my shoes and feel the rich earth beneath my feet. The soil felt as if you were stepping on soft piles of confectioner's sugar. It was a haven away from the city. To know that only one other family besides your own was living on that entire island was pretty unreal. You were entirely cut off from civilization once the tide went out. You might as well have been in a different country. The natural rhythm of the island would quiet your mind, and soon thoughts of the city were distant memories.

When I think back, my first thought is waking up in my grandparents' house and hearing a symphony of birds outside my window. Being from New York, I was used to hearing non-stop traffic at all hours and had no problem falling to sleep or waking up to all that noise. It was something quite different to fall asleep to absolute silence and then to hear so many different birds call to each other at the wee hours of the morning. I would wait and listen for the call of the bobwhite quail before I arose every morning. To me, the call of the bobwhite was Spring Island. We could always count on hearing and seeing them around our house. It wasn't unusual to see a hen and her chicks scurry across our path on the way to the skeet field or down to the pool. They were dear little birds, and just as the plantation days are gone forever, so sadly are the calls of the bobwhites.

One day my sister Kitty and I decided to go swimming. As we glanced at the water, we noticed an odd pattern of black dots scattered across the bottom of the pool. We didn't give it much thought at the time and spread out our towels and prepared to get some sun. It wasn't long before we heard the sound of shotguns from the skeet field, and then we felt the most intense stinging of what felt like hundreds of bees. We jumped off the towels and realized that the stinging came from the tiny black pellets now covering our towels. We heard the next round go off and dashed for cover but not before seeing a black cloud of shot sailing over the treetops toward us. It appeared that whoever had the brilliant idea of putting the skeet field near the swimming pool hadn't thought through the results.

Alligators have always lived on Spring Island, and I hope they always will. If you have a fear of these creatures, then Spring Island is not where you should hang your hat. A visit wasn't complete without at least one sighting of those prehistoric creatures. It wasn't unusual to approach the bream pond and hear a giant splash the closer you got. Sure enough, there was the telltale imprint of an alligator sunning itself before it was so rudely interrupted. I recall one time almost stepping on one before we each saw the other, and it slowly dropped back into the water.

One day, a group of us went down to the dock to swim in the river. I wasn't entirely keen on the idea, having never been in the river before, but not wanting to appear to be a party pooper I went along. It was a lot of fun although a bit unnerving not being able to see the river's bottom through all the mud

The Hays sisters, Betsy (Elizabeth) and Kitty (Katharine), with Marion Cooler in the background.

and muck. We would float along with the current for a while and then some alert child would call out "Swim back" and we'd make our way back toward the dock before we were carried too far away.

The next morning we had to return to New York, and as the *Gobbler* made its way across the river, I heard Gordon start to call my name and gesticulate wildly toward the back of the boat. I was not getting the gist of this pantomimed conversation and shrugged my shoulders. Gordon took the wheel and turned that boat around so fast that my family and I almost fell right into the river. As we approached the object he was pointing to, I realized I was staring down at the largest alligator I had ever seen. Not even twenty-four hours earlier, I had been floating in that exact location, not having given the least thought to alligators. Gordon's whoops of laughter serenaded us all the way to the main dock.

One evening it was decided that my father and I would be going out duck hunting the next morning and we needed to be up bright and early. This would be my first time duck hunting, and I was wildly excited. After getting on as many layers as possible under our waders, we set out in the dark of the early morning. I remember trying desperately not to splash any water. I am short and the water came to one inch below the top of the waders. It was an agonizingly slow wade out to the duck blind, but with the help and patience of my father and Gordon, we were soon settled in our little blind.

The morning was exceedingly cold, and I didn't wear gloves so that my hands would be ready to engage the gun. As we waited, our eyes adjusted to the dark and we could slowly make out the area around the blind. I'll never forget the beauty of that morning. The sky went from brilliant red, to pink,

to gold. The air was crisp, and as we waited, the first golden beams of sunlight slowly crept across the frost-covered corn stalks sticking up out of the water. It was glorious and so peaceful. I just watched in awe as the day unfolded.

It finally dawned on my father and me that we had yet to see one duck. We waited and muttered that it would be just our luck if the ducks had flown farther south to avoid this bitterly cold morning. We were about ready to pack it in when the loudest sound of flapping wings, splashing, and quacking startled us out of our frozen ponderings. By this time, our hands were numb and trying to snap the guns shut was a frustrating endeavor, but we managed. The sky was literally black with ducks and they gracefully sailed above us, in front of us, and behind our blind. As I am not one to brag, I'll let you guess how many we bagged that day.

My grandmother's life revolved around the hunting season. As she grew older, she spent more and more of her time on Spring Island. As I grew older, I would join in on some of the hunting. We never left the island without at least one cooler stuffed with quail, shrimp, duck, venison, and a giant box of pecans. By the time we got home to New York, and later Massachusetts, the cooler would invariably be a leaking mess, but we always got it to the freezer in time. I'd like to see people try and get a duct-taped Styrofoam cooler on a plane today.

I feel extraordinarily lucky to have experienced Spring Island during the plantation years. Its natural beauty was breathtaking and unlike any place I've been to since. I learned many of life's lessons from Spring Island, and I am grateful for the many happy memories this island gave to my family and me.

Betsy Hays and Gordon Mobley.

Kirke Thieriot Hall
Westwood, Massachusetts

When I think about Spring Island, my memories are filled with the sights and smells of childhood pleasures discovered in a faraway, remote part of the world that seemed a mysterious and totally different country from the one I knew back in Boston. South Carolina was an enigma, boasting beautiful, stately manor homes and yet filled with grocery stores with unrefined names like the Piggly Wiggly. Her heritage and culture were both rich and sophisticated, and at the same time, blue-collared and poor. There were always discoveries and adventures in store for me on my visits to my grandparents' plantation island.

A trip to Spring Island for our family meant an overnight train ride on Amtrak. (I used to think my parents thought it was the more luxurious way to travel, but little did I realize that it was because my mother preferred not to fly.) Upon arrival at the dock in the Chechessee community, we could immediately taste the humid, sweet air, ripe with the smells that low tide brings. Memories of island visits as a child were indulgences in all the five senses. There was the crisp, crunching sound of broken shells underfoot as we wandered among the Tabby Ruins; the bumpy, jostling horse and buggy rides out into the plantation fields; the high-pitched yelps of the hunt hounds as they dashed into the underbrush to retrieve their masters' fallen game birds; the damp, humid air that made it hard to breath when we jumped on my friend Pete Mobley's trampoline for hours at a time; the salty, smoky smell of a crab boil cooking outside in a metal garbage pail; the tickling sensation of our Spanish moss mustaches; the vibrant pink and orange colors of the setting sun over the marsh; the smooth, slimy feel of dozens of wriggling, live shrimp we pulled up in nets off the dock; and the comfort of Flowers' (my grandmother's cook) good ol' Southern cooking. (Her banana cream pudding—straight off the back of the Nilla Wafer box—still brings back warm and fuzzy feelings.)

It was *hot* during the summer in South Carolina, so hot that as a teenager I preferred to spend the daylight hours indoors in the air conditioning, as I found the humidity stifling. Even the water in the pool was too warm to be of any cooling comfort. Only the evening's gentle breezes could bring some relief, that is, until the mosquitoes discovered you. Sometimes it seemed unthinkable to actually head to the barn in the scorching sun to saddle up a horse for a trail ride, but we did. There was excitement to be had on that little island, and not even the fear of melting under the blazing sun could stop us from our adventures. At night we'd take our shotguns and pile into the Jeeps, switch on the blinding spotlights, and tear off into the dark in search of coons and possums to hunt. We'd bump and bounce as we went off-roading in the woods, following anything that moved. And of course the famous crab boils at the Gazebo were the highlight of our stay. I ate food I never saw on menus in restaurants back home. I saw animals and wild and beautiful birds I'd only seen previously in books. I shot off my first shotgun and can still recall the pain in my shoulder from its kickback. And it was there I tasted the thrill of freedom as I learned to drive a car (or Jeep, rather) as a budding teenager. I spent a day in the fifth grade at the local school in Beaufort with my friend Pete who lived on the island with her father and sisters. What a different life she and her friends led—their passion for cheerleading and beauty pageants fascinated me, as it was foreign compared with my sports and Girl Scouting.

My most special memory is, of course, my mother and stepfather's wedding when I was six. My brother and I participated in the ceremony and, together with relatives and friends, stood outdoors on the steps of the St. Francis of Assisi statue and embraced the beginning of a new life together. My trips to Spring Island taught me much about my family and my heritage—who my grandparents were (he died when I was a baby and she when I was twelve) and how they lived, who my mom was as their daughter, and what place I have in their family. Our family has a rich heritage and there is no denying that a special little plantation called Spring Island had much to do with its cultivation.

George Fiske and Elaine Walker walking up to their marriage ceremony at St. Francis with her children by her first marriage, Tyler and Kirke Hoffman, March 19, 1977.

159

Mark Sanford
Governor of South Carolina
Columbia, South Carolina

I apologize for the late note, but as you might imagine, I have been a bit jammed with this current endeavor.

Two memories jump out. One was when my sister, of all folks, shot her first deer at Spring Island and we had gone over to spend the night and deer hunt. Seems like we stayed in some barn or some fairly simple setting, but it was a big to do for us at the time, being high school and junior high school students. It seemed like we took the Bronco over on the barge. I remember it all being quite involved.

The larger thing that I remember is being over there for dove shoots. You'd be there for the shoot and have drinks up at Walker house. Then the question was the last boat out—early boat or last boat?

I remember being there on a January night. It was cold. You could see your breath, and you'd get into the boat. Gordon would be driving, and my dad and Henry Smythe and the other "grown-ups" would be standing. My brothers and I would be in the back part of the boat clutching a Lab for warmth and security. You would look behind you at this green phosphorous trail from the phosphorous in the water. You would look up and see the stars, and you would see more or less nothing on either side of you other than blackness and marsh grass whizzing by. What was most magical was looking at one of the grown-ups smoking a cigar and telling some story about a hunt.

There was just something magical about the passage from the island back to the mainland. It may have been only a mile but it seemed like a thousand miles. That sense of remoteness and the differentiating element with the boat ride used to get us more excited than anything else about our pilgrimage to Spring Island.

One thing that also stood out about Spring Island hunts was Gordon coming by and offering a cold Coke or Sprite, which for my brothers and me was a very big deal as I remember it.

I can't thank you enough for the warm memories that I do have of your spectacular spot.

Mark Sanford in his younger days (in black sweater) surrounded by admiring group of future voters at crab boil: John Sanford, Warren Mobley, Donna Mobley, and Pete Mobley. Gordon Mobley stands at left.

Margaret "Peggy" Sanford Peyton
Beaufort, South Carolina

Spring Island brings back so many wonderful memories, though my first experience there was traumatic. My husband, Marshall, was mesmerized by the island and its beauty, its situation on the river, its island mystique, its high land and magnificent live oak trees, and, of course, its great hunting potential. He first saw it in the mid-sixties when it was up for sale, and insisted that I had to see it too.

We made our trip to Spring Island a family excursion with our two little boys, Mark and Billy, leaving baby Sarah with a new baby sitter. A kindly soul from Lemon Island rented us a johnboat and off we went on our great adventure. A few minutes later, we were hung up on a sand bar. We had to keep ahead of the tide, so I had to jump out and help Marshall pull us across the bar. When finally free, we were able to find and tie up to the rickety dock at the Copp House.

We spent the afternoon tramping and exploring the area and the dilapidated structure. The boys loved it. Marshall was enchanted. I was overwhelmed, worried about Sarah with an unknown sitter, worn out from pushing the boat and tramping through the wilderness, and more than anything, overwhelmed with the enormity of the whole scene. What would we—could we—possibly do with an island of several thousand acres with no bridge and no phone? Logistically a nightmare! All I could think was that this island deserved someone who would understand it, love it, nurture it, and be enriched by it. Divine Providence intervened—a gentleman named Elisha Walker put in the high bid and walked away with the prize.

Later, we heard all about the wonderful things he was doing—bulldozers going twenty-four hours a day, clearing, cleaning, building roads and docks and even a garden for St. Francis. But we did not see the island until some years later, after he died.

Our friend from Sam's Point, Jim Rathbun, included us in his invitation to a dove shoot at Spring Island, saying that we had to meet Lucile Walker, a really wonderful lady. And indeed, she was a lovely lady. That was the beginning of a wonderful friendship. Lucile was so generous in sharing the island with her friends, and she included our whole family in many exciting events—dove shoots, deer hunts, lunches at the Gazebo. Just leaving the island in the boat with Gordon Mobley was a fantastic event in itself, filled with high spirits!

One particular occasion I remember well was a visit from our governor, Jim Edwards. Young Mark was with us as the helicopter landed and, along with Lucile, we greeted the governor. Afterwards, Mark excitedly told his little brothers and sister about the helicopter that landed right there in that field! But maybe it wasn't the helicopter that caught his attention that day—now I wonder if that was the event that planted a seed.

Most special was the annual opening of dove season on Labor Day weekend. What a splendid gathering of friends from Beaufort, Savannah, Charleston, and surrounding plantations. Lucile greeted us, and we all felt so fortunate to be there. What greater blessing could one have than an afternoon in the field at Spring Island, watching the birds fly, the dogs work, and enjoying the company of good friends?

Sarah Sanford, Marshall Sanford, Lucile Walker, Peggy Sanford, and John Sanford.

Sarah Sanford Rauch
Beaufort, South Carolina

There's nothing like sitting down on a cloudy Lowcountry day and taking the time to go back to a place and time that were so special in so many people's lives, especially the Sanfords' lives.

My father had a way of making everything into a tremendous adventure, and each time we went to Spring Island was a *huge* event for Dad. He used to say how lucky we all were to get to go to such an extraordinary place. And we knew it—only in our early adolescent minds, it would last forever. Yeah, it is special now, but nothing like it was as we knew it in its pristine state.

My most special moments include riding in the back of a pickup truck down that long dirt road and going by the Tabby Ruins and the statue of St. Francis. There they were, in a gorgeous clearing, surrounded by oaks, tangled vines, palmettos, snakes, and deer. And they were perfect right where they were.

I shot my first (okay, and *only* ever) deer on Spring Island. I must have been about fifteen years old and enough of a tomboy that everyone thought I was up to it, including me. After tears in the woods alone, I came out to a grinning Gordon Mobley, who made such an event of it all. Gordon seemed to have a way of making it better for me; he shored me up, and by the time we got back to the shed my dad and brothers already knew. That's when I learned about the tradition of "blooding" the face of a first-timer, and that's when I realized I was cut out for bird hunting and clay targets.

The dove shoots were always a big deal. I confess I remember more about the soda truck than I do the shooting. Gordon driving around offering Cokes in the field seemed to me to be the coolest thing. What luxury! Far more than the luxury, it was the camaraderie, the spirit of all the shoots at Spring Island. It must have been the combination of gathering for a boat ride over and then getting into the field knowing it would be a great shoot. And it always was, no matter what the weather or how many birds flew.

The boat rides over and back were as much an adventure as the visits. There was that great boathouse where everyone convened to wait for the boat to take them to the island. But this was no ordinary boathouse—there was the bar and those plastic "to-go cups" that had stenciled on them "One for the Road." My how times have changed! On the way in, everyone loaded into the boat with guns, dogs, children, and all the gear that goes with a shoot on an island. As we snaked our way from the mainland, my brothers and I would watch the water behind us, the wake spreading across the creek until it lapped onto the pluff mud on both sides at the same time.

My brothers and I were around during a heyday of shooting and outdoor adventure at Spring Island, so most of my memories stem from those activities. But even then, there were moments when we all stopped and looked at the island around us. None of us understood just how special the woods, fields, and waterways around the island really were. When I pause to think like this, I realize just how right my father was—we were immeasurably lucky to get to share that time in the history of such an extraordinary place. Spring Island was a place barely touched, adored by the few who got to visit. I was so young then, I really saw so little of what I now know was there. And even that little I did manage to see was more than anyone can imagine.

NAME	ADDRESS	DATE	
James B. Edwards Sr.	Columbia S.C.		Great hunt - Great Host
Jim Edwards Jr	800 Richland St	13 Sept 75	
Beaue Tyark	Beaufort		Wonderful Hunt
Mac McCarthy	Beaufort		Great Shoot
Edgar C. Glenn Jr	Beaufort, S.C.		great - as always
J.C. Myhh	Savannah, GA		Excellent Shoot.
Lavise + Joe Harrison	" "		ditto
Lewis M. Kalb Jr.	Columbia S.C.		Superb
R. T. Thompson, Jr.	Ridgeland, S.C.		Fantastic
Ray E. McLin Jr	Ridgeland, S.C.		A fine shoot
Betty + Lawrence Lee Jr	Savannah, Ga		Terrific !!
Jim Rantz	BEAUFORT S.C		
Allan McKenny	Sav'h - GA -		A cool Lou
Donald P. Pinckney	Bluffton SC.		Superb
A. H. Fickt	Ridgeland, S.C.		Superb
Moose McLin	Ridgeland, S.C.		A Great Hunt -
Dattie + Harold Floyd	Savannah, Ga.		Perfect day
Charles Jenkins	Beaufort S.C.		Beaut nice hunt
Jim Rantz	Beaufort S.C.		Great
Arthur Jenkins Jr.	Beaufort S.C.		A Great hunt
Jim Rathbun	Beaufort, S.C.		Great Hunt !?

A page from the Walker family's Spring Island Plantation guest book.

165

James B. Edwards
Former Governor of South Carolina
Mount Pleasant, South Carolina

My great and good friend, the late Beanie Trask, first introduced me to your parents and was the one that I frequently joined in the festivities of the occasions there. Beanie Trask and I had similar interests, mainly hunting and fishing. Your mother was very generous and kind and loved people, particularly people who had similar tastes. She enjoyed hunting as much as anyone I've known, but her interests were more in people.

Gordon Mobley and his family lived on the island, and he was a wonderful host to all your mother's friends. He took care of our every need in the field, and after the hunt he was always available to take us back to the mainland or fill any needs the guests had.

One of the memorable hunts we had was the time we were holding the Southern Governors' Conference on Hilton Head Island. Your mother heard about it and extended an invitation to shoot dove on Spring Island to any governors interested in doing so. Several of them joined me and it was a wonderful hunt with lots of shooting and full limits.

At the time, there was another Governor Edwards, who was governor of Louisiana. He enjoyed hunting very much and was a most colorful character. He had wonderful stories and was lots of fun to be with. Your mother and all the guests there were fascinated by him, and all the young ladies in the crowd were attracted to him, which was recipro-cated. He regaled us all with Cajun stories and tales of Louisiana politics. He was descended from the Huey P. Long-type.

Your mother enjoyed quail hunting, and she released quail on the island for all of her guests to hunt. We'd hunt out of the horse-drawn carriage, following the dogs until they pointed, and then we'd get out and shoot. On one occasion, our hunting party wound up at St. Francis of Assisi's statue and had a picnic lunch there. On another occasion I remember having a picnic lunch on the point overlooking the beautiful expanse of marsh and waterway where your mother had provided picnic tables and a shelter.

One of the many pleasant memories I have is gathering at the dock house on the mainland side before heading for the island. The refrigerator was always well stocked with any refreshment anyone would care for or need. We all frowned on participating in alcoholic beverages before the hunt, for obvious reasons. After the hunt, we would frequently stop by the dock house to discuss the activities of the day and enjoy the fellowship of the moment with appropriate libations. Most of the guests behaved themselves very well, and only on rare occasions did anyone over-participate.

All in all, my memories of the island and your mother and her many friends are pleasant and exciting. My only regret is that we can't enjoy her company again, but she will be remembered by all those who had the pleasure of her company and participated in sharing the hunting on this beautiful paradise of an island.

Opposite: Elaine & George Fiske, bride and groom, flanked by Governor and Mrs. James B. Edwards just after the governor performed the wedding ceremony, March 19, 1977.

Edward R. Greeff
Mill Neck, New York

One day, out riding for quail, it looked as if a dog was on point, but one of the other dogs shied. Gordon galloped up, got off the horse as fast as he could and grabbed the dog because the dog had found a rattler. He pulled the dog back, and then we shot the rattler. The speed with which Gordon jumped off the horse to grab the dog and save it from being struck by the rattler was amazing. He knew the movement the dog would make when he picked up the scent of the rattler.

Charles Meyer, Lucile Walker, Ed Greeff, and Betty Greeff.

168

Elrid Moody
Beaufort, South Carolina

Elisha and Lucile Walker came to Beaufort in 1964 to find an island to buy for a hunting retreat. They were staying at the Sea Island Motel.

A friend of mine happened to be having lunch at the Sea Island at the same time Mr. Walker was having lunch. My friend recognized Mr. Walker as a stranger in town. Therefore, being a "nosey" individual, he introduced himself and then began to "probe" the stranger.

Mr. Walker did not respond favorably to being questioned. However, he did say he was interested in buying an island without divulging which island.

My friend finished his lunch, and came immediately to see me at the Bank of Beaufort, of which I was president. He said I should arrange to meet Mr. Walker and gave me several reasons. Three reasons were: Mr. Walker appeared to be wealthy; second, he was planning to buy an island; and thirdly, he could be the vehicle whereby a revenue stream would materialize. These observations came true far beyond our fondest hope.

Most importantly, Mr. and Mrs. Elisha Walker became good citizens of the county and benefactors for many worthy causes. They were generous beyond measure in sharing the many pleasures to be found on Spring Island. The natural beauty, the dove hunting, quail hunting, wild hog hunting, duck hunting, oyster roasts, barbecues, trap and skeet shooting are a few of the fond memories persons from the area and others from far and wide have of Spring Island thanks to the bountiful and warm hospitality of Lucile and Elisha Walker.

At the time Mr. Walker was negotiating the purchase of Spring Island, he shared with me something of his plans. When he told me the price he was willing to pay, it seemed extravagant to me. I told Mr. Walker, "I don't know anything about your resources, but that is a heap of money!" We Southerners were born horse traders, and there were always at least two prices. You start off low and have in mind what you would really pay if push came to shove. Later, I learned that the final purchase price was about $400,000, not bad for a few weeks' work.

Mr. Walker located a jewel in Georgia, namely Gordon Mobley, who moved to Spring Island with his wife, Janice. They reared their family on Spring Island. Janice crossed the river by boat morning and evening, fair weather or foul, transporting their children to and from school. Their roots were sunk deep on Spring Island. Mr. Walker could not have found anyone to care for and love Spring Island more than Gordon and his family.

There were many "happenings" and events on Spring Island too numerous to recite. However, several are worthy of note.

An amusing incident occurred when Elisha received an invitation to an evening party in Beaufort. He told Gordon to have his boat, the *Gobbler*, ready for the trip to the mainland dock, and that they would probably not be returning until late that evening. By the time they arrived at the dock after the party, the sky was overcast, a heavy fog had rolled in, and there was no moonlight or starlight. Gordon suggested that they spend the night in the guest cottage on the mainland and cross the river in the morning. Elisha said, "No, I want to return to Spring Island tonight!" Gordon said he told himself, "He's the boss, it's his boat, so we'll go." They proceeded out into the river heading toward Spring

Island. Since the boat's spotlight could not penetrate the fog, travel was by instinct. Elisha told Gordon that he was headed toward the marsh and should go left. Gordon kept telling him to relax that they were still in the river channel, but to no avail. Gordon said that from Mr. Walker's voice, he had best go left, and within a few minutes, they ran hard aground. Elisha told Gordon to back up. Gordon told Elisha, "If I back up, the engine will pull mud through the exhaust." Elisha asked, "What do we do now?" Gordon replied that the tide was going out and that there was nothing to be done except to make themselves comfortable and wait for the incoming tide to float the boat. Gordon said that after that incident Elisha was more prone to take his advice on various occasions, especially when it came to running the river.

One of the most enjoyable events hosted by the Walkers on Spring Island was the annual Labor Day weekend deer drive. This event was a "conversation piece" throughout the year. Probably over a hundred persons gathered for this gala fest, including hunters, hunter-drivers, who brought their deer hounds to ferret out the deer, and a large contingent who came for the fellowship, Friday night poker games, and the telling of tall tales. The poker games were held in the tenant house by the grain bins and were a favorite of Lucile as she was an excellent poker player. There was keen competition for the position of "biggest tale spinner," more fondly referred to as the "biggest liar."

Saturday morning before daybreak, the hunters were dispersed throughout the woods on their deer stands. Gordon placed me in a choice location where deer frequently went to water. It was Gordon's custom to ride the woods in his pickup checking on the hunters. Twice Gordon came by my stand and discovered I was curled up in the ditch asleep. The second time, he said, "Come ride with me. You're a sorry hunter. You let a big buck almost step on you as he ran across the road." Thereafter, I rode with Gordon, which was my preference, as I did not wish to mar my record of never having killed a deer. Also, had I killed my first deer, the crowd gathered for lunch would have bloodied my face with my deer's blood. Even worse, had I missed the deer, they would have cut off the back of my shirttail.

Following lunch came the trial of those hunters who had killed their first deer and those who had shot at and missed a deer. A judge, a prosecutor, and an executioner were appointed. Those accused of missing a deer were called forth, witnesses requested, and the trials commenced. There was much jesting, with false accusations, denials, and attempts being made to escape the judgment. Lucile was usually the executioner who wielded the hunting knife and destroyed many LL Bean shirts. She entered into her role with gusto, and on a couple of occasions, nicked the flesh. Several hunters enthusiastically participated in the "face bloodying," especially when the victim happened to be a family member or a friend. A good time was enjoyed by all, and those who desired were the recipients of a package of venison.

Lucile Walker with arm on Gordon Mobley's shoulder as Elrid Moody looks on from behind them.

B Hutson
Charleston, South Carolina

Elliott and I enjoyed many memorable visits to Spring Island over the years. It was always nice to look forward to seeing Lucile and Elisha, plus seeing the beautiful unspoiled virgin forest and wetlands.

It is a gone-by treat to experience waking up in the morning to shoot ducks, have a sumptuous breakfast, and walk out of the door to see buggy and mules, dogs, horses, and guides for a wonderful experience of quail shooting. It was peace at an all-time high. The dogs were outstanding, and I might add Elliott could hit the birds, which made it even better!

We would convene at the attractive Gazebo in the woods for a delectable lunch of quail and red rice, and then back in the rig for a perfect afternoon of hunting. To me, the woods were always so fascinating and beautiful with so many different things taking place—fox, squirrels, Tabby Ruins, dove fields, duck ponds, etc. The birding was always excellent.

The company was always a good mix—Savannah, Charleston, and other parts of the Lowcountry. The boat trip over to the island was magical; you would always be off to a good start. Gordon was always the helpful and accommodating man in charge. He did a masterful job of carrying out the plans and responsibilities given to him.

I have spent some pretty hot September visits in the dove fields, but it was so refreshing to have a cool drink come by via guide in the middle of the afternoon when it was probably ninety degrees. The shooting was always excellent. Your parents had marvelous "big blinds" made from lots of bales of pine straw. We were always honored to be included and we loved it!

Elliott and I were very fond of your parents. Elliott had shown Elisha several other parcels of property before he bought the Spring Island tract. He made a good choice!

Every meal in the house was done well—simplicity at its best and so good. The house was so perfect with the Richard Bishop needlepoint around the clock and all the lovely Bishop prints. We had many, many fun times and are humbled by knowing Lucile and Elisha.

Writing this makes me feel very nostalgic. If we could only turn the clock back! We had some of the best times of our lives on Spring Island.

Arthur S. Jenkins, MD
Beaufort, South Carolina

While the Walker family was spending their later years at Spring Island, I had the privilege of helping care for their health problems, which were numerous and sometimes difficult.

Mr. Walker died on a visit to Mexico, apparently from chronic heart problems.

Lucile lived for nine more years and was determined to spend her last on Spring Island. This, of course, was complicated by the across-the-river transportation problem. So with the expert management of her devoted Gordon Mobley, we created a mini-intensive care unit at the Walker house, complete with oxygen, I.V. equipment, nurses, appropriate furniture, and me standing by when needed. On one occasion, I accompanied her by jet to Long Island.

Gordon's critical surveillance was responsible for the success of her survival. Unfortunately, she developed a disastrous problem requiring emergency surgery and succumbed post-operatively in Savannah.

The Weezie Foundation was a philanthropic organization established by the Walker family to benefit children. Weezie was a daughter who died in a tragic accident at ten years old. The family became interested in the Beaufort community and honored us with contributions of thousands of dollars, and honored me with the obligation of choosing recipients such as the Speech and Hearing Clinic, Beaufort Academy, hospital isolettes for newborns, monitoring equipment, and other grants, which continued even after Lucile's death.

My sons and I enjoyed Gordon's hospitality over the years until his unfortunate demise. Crab boils for friends were a classic event. Hunting was spectacular and often amusing. You could get your shirttail cut even if you were not hunting.

The wildlife representative visited frequently to collect deer specimens. One day, a hunter named Bob Lamar shot his first deer and, of course, got a bloody face. He grabbed a jar of clear fluid to wash it off. It turned out to be not water, but formaldehyde. This led to some anxious moments, but fortunately we quickly found some real water for a rinse and no serious harm done, only burning eyes.

I could go on and on but will close with that story. I very much appreciate all the courtesies and good times extended to the Jenkins family, which we will never forget.

Charles Jenkins, Jim Gray, Gordon Mobley, and Arthur Jenkins.

O. J. Small
Charleston, South Carolina

Perhaps my memory bank is a little faded at this time, but among my favorite memories is one that took place at Midway Plantation. Elisha had invited two Frenchmen to Spring Island, Pierre Charbonnet and Dr. Henry DuPuis, if my recollection is nearly right. He called to ask if I had ducks because Spring Island did not. Midway had a good quantity of ring-necks, so I asked him to bring them over Friday night for a Saturday morning shoot. As it turned out, my little cabin was fully occupied on this occasion.

It was a rainy evening and morning; still the hunt was splendid. My brother Robert's marksmanship seemed to impress the Frenchmen. During the cocktail hour Friday evening, we had some drop-in visitors, not entirely unexpected because they were shooting at a nearby plantation. Elisha's Labrador, Ring, was relaxed in front of the fire when Burnet Maybank, a visitor, exclaimed aloud, "I have been looking for a bitch to breed my Bullet to, but that Lab does not measure up."

Silence immediately overwhelmed the room. No interpretation was needed. Elisha was about to explode. Peace was restored when brother Robert exclaimed, "Now we know why Burnet did not make it in his campaign for governor!"

Mary Raht Smith
Charleston, South Carolina

In 1965, the Walkers had a man named Wallace Stacy living in the office apartment on the mainland, but he was not capable of handling the project that Elisha had in mind. My good friend Henry Smythe told me that he had a client who needed someone to help him develop an island that was pretty wild and turn it into the best shooting plantation in the South. Henry asked me to go up to Syosset to visit the Walkers for the weekend.

They had a lot of pictures of the island, and we stayed up half the night looking at them and talking about the project. We ended the weekend deciding to work together, but as we knew we would be social friends as well, we had an understanding that either one could part company with the business arrangement and still be friends.

John Carswell put Elisha up for membership in the Oglethorpe Club in Savannah. We could then order alcohol by the case from them, and Lucile and I had a good place to go when we were in the city shopping.

Early morning dove hunters at Tabby Ruins: Bill Hays, John Millington, and Clark Whitcomb.

James R. Davis
Savannah, Georgia

There was no summer so magical as that of 1965 which I spent on Spring Island. I was 17 years old and a fifth former at Canterbury School, a New England prep school. God was looking down on me favorably that year as Bayard Walker, nephew of Elisha Walker, became one of my two roommates. Our junior year progressed quickly. With summer approaching, Bayard had no job nor plans for that summer. Neither did I.

Mr. Walker had just purchased Spring Island and needed some laborers to start preparing the island for the many activities he envisioned. By early June, plane tickets were purchased for Savannah and we were on our way.

While we had no idea what kind of creature comforts would befall us, our trust in Mr. Walker was well founded. We were given exclusive rights to a new Land Rover, two Boston Whalers, and a quaint little cottage at Chechessee landing. For two New York City slickers who thought Central Park was the "country", we now thought we had died and gone to heaven.

Spring Island in 1965 was thousands of acres of dense, impenetrable jungle, so thick you couldn't walk straight for ten feet without running into an obstacle that necessitated a substantial by-pass. Much of our early work consisted of helping the resident engineer mark and flag roads as well as delineate food plots for what would become a burgeoning quail population.

Because the island had not been inhabited or hunted for years, it was overrun with feral hogs that ran in large packs. Even with the dense brush, it was not uncommon to see as many as a hundred hogs in a day. The story always lingered in the back of my mind of the man who years before had been attacked by hogs on the island and almost bled to death before he escaped back to the mainland.

Since quail and hogs are not compatible, Mr. Walker wanted the hogs eliminated. While he encouraged us to shoot as many as possible, he knew our efforts paled in the face of the rampant population. Before long a crew of "good ol' boys" with hounds were hired to eliminate the Spring Island hogs. Bayard and I had attached ourselves to this crew chasing the wild boars of Spring Island.

The standard operating procedure was to release the hounds into the woods; in short order they would be hot on the trail of a pack of hogs. Eventually the dogs would encircle a hog who was not happy with the circumstances. A cat-and-mouse game would ensue whereby dog and hog would lunge at each other at opposite times. The goal of the hog was to lower its head and try to impale the dog under its belly with its long tusks and then catapult the dog over its head. If the dog didn't jump back fast enough, it would end up flying through the air over the hog's back.

Over the summer we saw quite a few dogs get their stomachs ripped open and spew their entrails all over the ground. Inevitably, when being chased, the hogs always sought refuge in the thickest, boggiest swamp they could find. The ensuing battle resembled something between a cockfight and a mud-wrestling contest.

A dirtier job could not have been found anywhere. What happened at this point? Believe it or not, the tough part was yet to come. With the dogs in a pitched battle facing the hogs, one of the boys (let's assume his name was "Bubba") would try to sneak up behind the hog and grab its two hind legs in the hopes of rendering it immobile. At this point the hog's attention would turn to Bubba and another stand-off would ensue. If Bubba was fast enough, the hog would be swept off its feet and its hind legs tied up and bound. Then came the front legs. This did not differ much from the cattle roping you see at a rodeo except that the cows don't have six-inch tusks trying to cut you up. If the roping was successful, the last step was to cart the animal off the island and sell it at market.

This ordeal was so complicated and dangerous that I quickly surmised these hogs were worth more alive at market than dead as it would have been much easier simply to shoot them. I have had many opportunities to hunt wild boar in the following years, but I still marvel at the fearlessness of these "Bubbas" and the tenacity of their dogs, many of whom lost their lives in pursuit of the wild boar of Spring Island .

The only thing to impress us more that summer was an elite clique within that group of "hawg chasers" who brought over horses on barges from the mainland to chase the feral cattle that had lived on the island for decades. The riders had to get close enough to dart the animals with a tranquilizer gun. These cattle were wary and not fond of humans so they shot off into the woods at the first sight of a person. How those riders could ride through that dense jungle bare-chested at a full gallop chasing those cows in an effort to pull up alongside them and then shoot them with a dart gun is a feat that I will put up alongside the building of the pyramids anytime.

And speaking of wonders, Bayard and I were privileged that summer to experience that awe and sense of discovery that explorers feel when they make a new finding. I have visited the Aztec pyramids in the jungles of Honduras and the Yucatan, and it is with this same sense of bewilderment that we viewed Spring Island. One day while blazing a trail with our machetes through the jungles of Spring Island, we happened upon the Oak Avenue and the Tabby Ruins. The dense forest had reclaimed this area many decades ago so the under story of hardwoods made it difficult to ascertain whether we were seeing an oak avenue or a simple coincidental alignment of very mature oak trees. Regardless, the Tabby Ruins were self evident, and we spent days wondering about who had lived there, and when, and what had happened to these settlers.

Thank you, Mr. Walker, for the opportunity of a lifetime.

"Good ol' boys" hauling hog-tied wild boar out of the muck, 1965.

Robert Harrison
Savannah, Georgia

I did not come to the island very much until George and Elaine Fiske invited us in the '80s after your mother had passed away. Subsequently, John Carswell, Bill Sprague, and I bought Low Bottom from Mrs. Marshall Fields and traded it to Chaffin and Light for two founder lots on Spring Island. We then enjoyed four years of shooting visitations, met some of the new buyers, and enjoyed the company of the Mobleys and the exquisite beauty of the island. I was also active in promoting the development in the beginning as a founder.

My parents, of course, came to the island often and enjoyed their visits immensely. The dove and quail shoots they enjoyed were legendary. There are two things I do remember my father telling me.

One year your father brought in and raised 325 semi-wild mallards, which he hoped would grow up and provide shooting during the season. One day, they got up off the pond and every single one flew off, never to return. None was shot. A band from one was discovered the next year in Arkansas.

The other story was about the old Copp House near where the Gazebo is. Gordon actually told me that your parents were outside the old home having a picnic one day and your father related that he would like to repair the house and have it as the main house for the island. Your mother was not excited about the idea; your father quietly told Gordon to demolish the house and that he did not want to see it on his next visit. Accordingly, Gordon made it "disappear" such that when your father returned to the island sometime later, it was gone. Thence came what we all have known as the "Walker House" at the other end of the island.

Elisha Walker (third from right, smiling) picnicking with friends at the Copp House before it disappeared, 1967. Left to right: Jane & Dick Benziger, Elie Reichner, Elisha & Lucile Walker, and Mary Raht.

John Millington
Washington, Connecticut

I have so many wonderful memories of Spring Island that I hardly know where to begin. Maybe it's at the breakfast table with that view out over the water, the carved birds, and the hilarious conversations, or learning to throw a shrimp net while at the same time keeping our front teeth intact. Or in the field, with that magic word "Point!" and the rush of having those birds flush, with dogs and handlers doing all the right things.

And while we're on the subject of quail, I see in my mind's eye a covey rising, and you, Lucile, taking out a bird on the rise, and Gordon so proud of your shot, as we all were. I'm remembering two instances of this: one in one of the inside fields; the other, far more historic, for it occurred on the fields that abut the Tabby Ruins. And this, as I remember it, was the last time I heard anyone shoot at Spring Island. What a conclusion!

Another special event, my first crab boil: the newspapers spread across the dinner table, empty beer bottles at the ready, and gallons of crabs, sausages, onions, potatoes, etc., all dumped in front of the eight or ten of us who graced that Thanksgiving table. Then the smashing of the claws and the sucking sounds as you drained the last remnants, finished off by an enormous wiener schnitzel. All

this captained by dear Gordon, SaSa, and Pete. What memories!

But above all, perhaps, it was those dove shoots. And one in particular, at the Tabby Ruins. I don't think I have ever had shooting like that. Birds wheeling in at sixty and seventy miles an hour from every direction—so fast, so many times, that you could only spot shoot. But hit or miss, the beauty of those historic tabbies, with the sun coming up to light the marsh beyond, and the glorious quail fields—what a time!

And a particular episode saw me needing to stand a bit higher along a fence line, so I clambered atop a small mound and watched the birds flying. As I shot, I felt a little pinch in my right calf. I didn't pay much attention, and shot again, and a couple of more pinches. And the next thing I knew, ladies and gentlemen, I was on fire. My precious mound was the home of ten million fire ants. You have never seen anybody undress quite as fast as I did. Right down to the buff. And if you thought I cared whether there were any ladies present, you were wrong!

The long and the short of it is that memory stayed with me in a very tangible way until the festering of the fire ant attack went away. But even those could in no way daunt what was so magnificent an afternoon.

Thank you again, dear Hayses, for these and so many more glorious memories of Spring Island.

Opposite: John Millington; Edwina Millington.

Nancy and Clark Whitcomb
Nantucket, Massachusetts

Icy Duck Hunting. Our first visit to Spring Island, New Year's weekend sometime around 1980, was during one of the coldest winters on record. Even the fountain in front of the Walker House was frozen. That didn't stop Gordon from putting Lucile and Clark into duck blinds in the flooded cornfields. Icicles dripping off of parka hoods and slipping and sliding on the floor of the duck blind did not dampen our enthusiasm for the hunt, but our body temperatures were severely compromised.

Missed Opportunities. Clark's lingering embarrassment over his lack of wing-shooting accuracy was further heightened when several widgeons presented themselves as if hanging from sky hooks over the decoys in front of the duck blind on Pine Island Pond. Gordon had set Clark up in this prime spot and gone about his business elsewhere, only to sneak in just as the widgeons flew into the decoys. He was witness to a shotgun barrage that left multiple holes in the sky and the widgeons flying free. Clark still remembers his own red face and Gordon's good-natured smirk.

Clark and His Faithful Pointer at One of the Last Great Dove Shoots. Plantation owners flocked to Spring Island for one of the last big dove shoots hosted by Lucile and Bill. Placed strategically around grain fields, the hunters waited for the unsuspecting dove (which had been scared up by Gordon, Joe, William, and their honking horns) to fly across their battle stations. Cries of "Mark!" echoed across the field followed by shotgun reports. Nancy, the non-shooter, was given huge responsibility to point in the right direction and retrieve the poor fallen birds.

Oyster Roasts at the Gazebo. These luncheons meant total abandonment of dignity and good manners. Oysters grilled on the open fire, quail and red beans and corn bread and various potables ruined any plans for strenuous activities for the rest of the day.

"Ge' Ou' the Road"—Gordon's Dog and Nancy's Commands. We were often blessed to watch Gordon as master of the hunt command his dogs (Jet, Rebel). One of his loudest cries to these enthusiastic canines

Left: Frozen fountain at Walker House on icy winter morning.

Opposite: Clark Whitcomb with his "pointer," Nancy Whitcomb.

was "Ge' ou' the road." One mini-quail shoot, Nancy, as non–shooter, was conscripted to drive the pickup truck. Gordon, riding on the back bumper, was choreographing the hunt. When he yelled his command, Nancy responded by promptly driving the truck off the road. Good dog, Nancy.

James and the Biting Horse. During a day's quail shoot, James, one of the bush beaters, was bitten significantly in his privates by an ill-tempered nag.

The visit to the hospital, as told by Gordon, was good theater, at James' expense. When the admitting nurse asked what the problem was, James couldn't articulate the details. Gordon acted as translator, urging James to forget his very determined modesty. After resultant treatment, whatever that entailed, James was back in operation, so to speak, the next day.

Marion and the Mules. One of the benefits of being the only non-shooter in these wonderful visits to

Nancy & Clark Whitcomb at skeet range.

Spring Island, Nancy remembers so fondly, were the long hours sitting on the wagon's front bench with Marion as he drove the mule wagon, some dogs at our feet, and others whimpering with excitement in the back. The hunters were engaged in frenzied activity, and she and Marion chatted in quiet companionship. Those were wonderful days!

Lee and Cheese Grits. Lee's countless meals served at the round table are lingering memories. We remember broccoli salad, soufflé, duck breasts, quail and dove, crab cakes, and Lee's wry humor.

Crab Boils and Gluttony. Every trip to Spring Island included a crab boil at Gordon's house. We will never forget our first experience of watching newspaper being laid as the tablecloth, Coke bottles and paper towels set out as the table setting, and Gordon bringing in the huge kettle and pouring its contents across the center of the table. Out came crabs, corn, onions, and kielbasa, all of which we attacked with our hands. Learning to make an "ice cream cone" out of the crab legs is one of life's finest lessons!

Connie Trask
Beaufort, South Carolina

Lucile and Bill Hays shared Spring Island with many people and many times included our family. One time when my husband, George, could not come because he had some work to do in Beaufort, I went alone. The entire group for that day was stunned that George had decided to stay in Beaufort. Robbie Harrison said that people would travel from the far side of the world to take part in what Spring Island offered, and there was George over in Beaufort *working*.

The next hunt George was there along with our two sons, Christian and Graham, who were nine and ten years old. These young boys had not been able to grow up hunting as we had lived in Atlanta many of those years. When we did move back to the Low-country they were eager and ready to improve their hunting skills and loved going to Spring Island.

I also needed to learn to shoot, and once I learned I needed lots of improvement. Everyone was sweet, encouraging, and patient with me, but it was on Spring Island that the truth finally hit home. It was a wonderful day and a beautiful dove hunt. George may have been out in the field reading a novel, something he often did on these hunts while his wife and sons were trying to bring home dinner. I had hit a dove and went out in the field to pick it up. I was carrying my gun under my arm with the barrel pointing down to the ground. I leaned over, picked up my bird, and went back to my place for my next shot, hoping to add another bird to my bag.

When I shot this time I heard a strange noise and looked at my barrel which had peeled like a banana half way down. Sandy soil had gotten into the bar-

rel when I bent down minutes earlier to pick up my bird, but I had not realized it.

It was then that I along with my family decided that the best place for my gun was on the wall. I had to agree with them. I knew that Lucile and Bill would still want me to come to Spring Island with my family. I could still take part in the bringing together of wonderful people and good times, but I would have to leave my gun on the wall.

George Trask on horseback at quail hunt.

185

Ben Moore
Charleston, South Carolina

My law partner, Henry Smythe, was retained by the Sherman and Sterling law firm in New York to represent the interests of Elisha Walker of New York when he purchased Spring Island in the 1960s. In addition to being an outstanding lawyer in the real estate field, Henry Smythe was arguably the finest non-professional outdoorsman I have ever known. He grew up hunting everything that was to be hunted in the South Carolina Lowcountry: deer (his passion), ducks, quail, dove, and turkeys. He was also an enthusiastic fisherman, both saltwater and freshwater, making annual trips to the Restigouche River for Atlantic salmon.

I suspect that when he first met Mr. Walker on Spring Island, and was given a tour, he experienced a sort of nirvana. The woods, the fields, the waters, all were at the center of Henry's outdoor universe. My recollection is that Henry and Elisha Walker quickly became friends and Mr. Walker soon realized what a sportsman Henry was. As a result, Henry was invited to participate in deer drives, turkey hunts, quail shoots, and dove hunts. Given the opportunity, Henry would take along with him his close friend, Elliott Hutson, who was also instrumental in Mr. Walker's purchase of Spring Island. In due course, Henry also arranged for his good Charleston friend, Mary Raht, to become the social secretary of the Walkers at Spring Island. Henry also became a close friend of Gordon Mobley, the manager of Spring Island Plantation.

It was through Henry that I was first invited to Spring Island, but I did not know Mr. Walker. I met Mrs. Lucile Walker sometime after Mr. Walker's death, and I like to think that we became friends. My first few visits were always to hunt deer during the fall, when the island was particularly lovely. Later, I was invited on dove shoots, which were some of the best I have ever known. It was during those pleasant years that I first met and became friends with Lucile Hays and Elaine Fiske and spent many pleasant hours with them. The cocktail parties after the hunts were always delightful as were the two or three occasions when Eleanor and I were invited to spend the night at the Spring Island house.

Although Spring Island has been developed and we have spent many pleasant hours there with friends, it is nonetheless a shame that the island could not have been maintained in its pristine beauty. I recognize that modern economics makes such a venture enormously difficult. The same situation occurred with the family that owned Kiawah Island, which sold out to the Kuwaitis in 1974. But the memories remain, and Thomas More might have said it best:

> *When Time who steals our years away,*
> *Shall steal our pleasures too,*
> *The mem'ry of the past will stay,*
> *And half our joys renew.*

Opposite: At the end of the day: Marion Cooler, William Fripp, and Collins Mitchell with the mule-drawn wagon.

Ned Morgens
First Non-Family Renter
of Spring Island Plantation for Quail Hunting
Norwalk, Connecticut

I remember the ice water. Gordon never drank coffee that we knew of, and when he woke us that first morning he had a glass if ice water in hand. It was 5 a.m. and still dark as we pulled our gear and ourselves together for a duck hunt. None of us had yet seen the island in daylight.

I think it was Robbie Harrison of Savannah or the late Bill Baldwin of Charleston who tipped us off that the Walker family was willing to rent Spring Island to a few parties of four or six for a week of quail, duck, and dove shooting. Having seen Lowcountry spots like Bull Island and Davant Plantation near Ridgeland, we signed on, sight unseen.

In total darkness, Gordon Mobley's brother Joe led Linda and me out through knee-deep water to one of the blinds in the wood-duck ponds and, along with his flashlight, disappeared back into the night. The deep silence was broken by an owl now and then and the tantalizing "weep, weep, weep" of wood ducks on the wing. Dawn came like creation. Slowly, shapes emerged to eyes without preconception of what would come. It is a magic moment for both of us to this day.

It was the early '80s when we first came; time is hard on precise memory. There was a dock at the little settlement of Chechessee and another near the Walker House. Gordon picked us up after dark and navigated the oyster shoals at high speed. The roads were sand tracks and few in number; moving around was mostly on horseback or mule wagon. Each day the wagon and the saddle horses pulled up in the circle behind the Walker House at eight o'clock sharp, dogs barking to get going and riders adjusting stirrups, equally eager.

Lunch was afield, sometimes at the Gazebo or on Pine Island—hot soup, cold quail, roasted oysters, and sweet tea. If the shooting was over for the day, you would wash it down with ice-cold beer or crisp white wine. The oyster roasts and crab boils behind the Walker House or at Gordon's little house near the dock were filled with noisy chatter about dogs and ducks and birds we should have hit. The stars come out early at Spring Island in winter, and the group fell into silent awe as we walked back toward beckoning beds.

We never met the Walkers or thanked them for carving a paradise out of the jungle they must have found, but judging from their offspring, we would have enjoyed their friendship.

Opposite: Tabby Ruins from afar (photograph by Jane Sampson).

189

Opposite: View toward Port Royal Sound from Tabby Ruins (photograph by Jane Sampson).

Epilogue

Those Were the Days

Quiet shadows down tree-lined drive
that point the way to warmth and love
added to food as if prepared from above.
Those were the days— they'll always be alive.

Pecan grove with dove overhead,
long-stemmed pines to rule their flight.
Tabby Ruins with birds in morning's flight.
Those were the days on our memories fed.

From haunting sound of bobwhite call
to trembling pointer marking covey's place
with explosion of wings as off they race.
Those were the days, oh what a ball!

These are the treasures greater than gold,
for they are endless in their recall
whether in winter, spring, or fall.
Those were the days, a gift forever to behold.

Thus, there could be no finer host;
for all they've given us four,
we raise our glasses in salute at the door.
For those were the days—a final Spring Island toast.

John Millington

Tabby Ruins in the fog (photograph by Peggy Hendrick).

Following Elisha's death, the island passed in due course into other hands. It was fortunate for Spring Island that the new owners, Jim Light and Betsy and Jim Chaffin and the group they put together, are both loving and caring. They converted a paradise for a few fortunate individuals into a resort, and in the process managed to preserve as much of the natural beauty as possible.

The Arnold Palmer golf course has added new vistas of the river and allowed some of the majestic live oaks to emerge from the forest and stand guard along the fairways and behind the greens. The sun still sets over the river flowing gently around the island; the birds are still singing their songs; the ducks and geese still swoop down out of the sky and splash into the ponds at sunrise and announce their departure at sunset with loud squawking; the deer still peer nervously around and dash away at the slightest sound; the dirt roads have, for the most part, been left unpaved.

St. Francis still gazes serenely down the lane of live oaks to the Tabby Ruins and the river beyond; the lodge and the Gazebo still offer a warm and blissful welcome to all who come to enjoy a few enchanting hours in these wonderful places.

In short, despite the attractive new homes that have arisen from the wilderness, it is still Elisha's island. I truly believe that if Elisha were to fly down from heaven to take a look around, he would be both happy and proud at what he saw.

D. Nelson Adams

Sunset at Spring Island Plantation (photograph by Jane Sampson).

Acknowledgments

WARM THANKS to my sister, Elaine, for writing about our family logo and for Jane Sampson's pictures. Both are very important to the book, and I am so happy you are a part of this project. My family have all been so supportive, especially my husband, Bill. He has listened endlessly to, "Does this sound all right?" He has been number-one editor and I appreciate his patience. Thank you to my daughters, Kitty and Betsy, for their enthusiasm, encouragement, and writings. I thank my niece, Kirke Thieriot Hall, my cousin Bayard Walker, and his friend Jim Davis.

A very special thank you goes to Nelson Adams, my father's lifelong friend, lawyer, and advisor. You were a part of our Spring Island experience from beginning to end.

The Mobley family helped create an important part of this book. Thank you Janice, Donna, SaSa, and Pete for your fine work as I know it was not easy.

I appreciate all the memories, both oral and written, given to me by others. They illustrate how special Spring Island was to all who knew it during the Walker years. To John Carswell, thank you for providing information not otherwise available to me. And to all my other writers, grateful thanks. Each and every one of you has given a different perspective or story that has created a well-rounded "Remembrance" of my family's years on Spring Island.

To my editor, Barbara Martin, a huge thank you for spending every Wednesday last winter at Spring Island with me. I loved working with you, and you helped make it easy.

My most heartfelt thanks to George Trask, my publisher. As he and his wife, Connie, are friends who had often visited Spring Island, he had the vision to see what this book could and should be. I envisioned a paperback with a few pictures; he envisioned this beautiful coffee-table book. Thank you, thank you, George, for your friendship, perseverance, and expertise.

Lucile Walker Hays
Nantucket Island, Massachusetts
July 18, 2004

Colophon

Tabby Manse

Coastal Villages Press is dedicated to helping
to preserve the timeless values of traditional
places along America's Atlantic coast—
building houses to endure through
the centuries; living in harmony
with the natural environment;
honoring history, culture,
family and friends—
and helping to
make
these
values
relevant
today.
This
book
was
completed
on August 3, 2004, in Stonington, Maine. It was
designed and set by George Graham Trask in Bembo,
a typeface inspired by the Italian renaissance.